TESTIMONIALS

Leadership is about inspiring and motivating others and the key to working with humans is firstly recognising they are all different individuals and what that means is that as a leader you must adapt!!! *Leading Excellence* truly taps into what it takes to be a leader who adapts to the changing needs of others and provides very practical and easy to apply lessons that help a leader to identify what they need to do to respond to the ever evolving needs of their team and the business and context in which they are operating. What I loved about this book was the real life case studies that show, not only how The 5 Hats of the Adaptive Leader can provide a real step change in your leadership, but the book does not shy away from calling out the behaviours that need to change and the difficult parts that come with leadership. This is a no-nonsense guide that holds the mirror up to the reader and invites them to reflect on their own leadership and then take the steps to change what is necessary.

Nadine Brennan Manager Global Leadership Development, BHP

Leading Excellence provides great insight into the foundation leadership qualities. Whether an experienced leader or wanting to broaden your knowledge base, reading this book will give you different insights that will no doubt further your leadership abilities. I thoroughly enjoyed the read and would recommend it to anyone wanting to extend their leadership knowledge and abilities personally and professionally.

Nathan Charles Executive General Manager Sydney University Football Club.2014/15 Wallaby, Western Force and Melbourne Rebels Super Rugby

There are thousands of books written on the subject of 'Leadership.' Most of these books talk about theory and leave little to practical implementation. *Leading Excellence* debunks this notion by offering a hands-on process to become an 'Adaptive Leader.' Leadership is not telling others what to do. It inspires others to work together for the common good of all stakeholders. However, inspiration (the first of the '5 Hats') is insufficient by itself. A leader must ensure that the framework is set for others to succeed. The 5 Hats of the Adaptive Leader does just that by providing a practical 5-Step process to win. Peppered with insightful case studies, the authors bring a reality to the subject of leadership. This book separates itself from the leadership pollution in the marketplace today. To call this a 'book' may be a disservice to the authors, as I feel it is a hands-on manual that should be read (and implemented) by anyone in a leadership position or by those aspiring for leadership roles.

Mark DeLuzio President & CEO of Lean Horizons Consulting, LLC, known as a pioneer of Lean and the principal architect of the Danaher Business System (DBS).

Leading Excellence is a must read for any leader or aspiring leader no matter what type of organisation they are in. Whether that's the corporate, sporting or not-for-profit world, this book provides a framework and gives a hands-on practical guide to help leaders develop their skills to help drive a high performing sustainable culture in the organisation, through leading by example, collaboration and teamwork. There are many leadership books out there, however, this one gives the reader a step-by-step guide on how to be more effective as an adaptive leader.

Pádraig Harrington Ryder Cup Captain, 3-time major champion and 2024 World Golf Hall of Fame

At last, a simple to understand book about leadership. The 5 hats approach to adaptive leadership is easy to grasp and is illustrated with a series of cases and personal anecdotes from the authors. The book has been inspired by thinking from the Shingo Institute and puts the receiver of the leadership at the heart of the given approach. It is a great starting point for those moving into a leadership role as well as those looking to develop themselves into a great leader.

Professor Peter Hines Enterprise Excellence Network

A 'Win-Win'. *Leading Excellence* is a must read for any leader wanting to improve their effectiveness. There are great books on organisational leadership, but this one fills a gap as a resource for 'Individual Leadership'. The practical, 'how to' principle-based steps including actions and behaviours will improve your relationship with those your lead and serve. It will also render the business results that you and your organisation need.

Mike Hoseus Co Author of Shingo Award winning book Toyota Culture, Executive Director, Center for Quality People and Organisations, Former Executive Toyota Motor Manufacturing

A compelling read for developing and emerging leaders based on real life situations, experiences and outcomes. Highly recommended.

Tony Howarth AO, CitWA, Hon LLD (UWA), SF Fin(Life), FAICD(Life). Chairman Alinta Energy

The power of this book, *Leading Excellence*, truly resonates with you, it both supports your own knowledge, but challenges you to also grow through the insightful structure, to know your own true purpose and how to develop others as part of what true leaders must do every day. Its relevancy comes through respecting how it is written, by Leaders of Practiced and Life Experiences, with purpose, insight and currentness in Leading Excellence.

Leadership is about developing others and being self-aware that we were gifted Two ears, two eyes and one mouth that suggests we reflect on using them proportionally, and that as we walk through our own environments every day, be conscious of our shadow of leadership is being followed even as we walk away, Leaders are continually observed and their behaviours reflected. A book that creates a mind shift to challenge how we build appropriate Cultures that will sustain is a refreshing and powerful read, that should make many Leaders look in the mirror and see how many hats they have truly mastered and be mindful of how they impact others.

Kieran Noonan Shingo Institute Executive Board Member, Chairman of the Irish Centre for Business Excellence, Abbott Global Operations & Opex Leader.

This book provides leaders an inspiring playbook to navigate an increasing volatile and complex environment to drive next level impact and results.

Justin Scanlan, Managing Partner, Deloitte Consulting Western Australia

Healthcare is arguably the most complex sociotechnical system on the planet. Yet, we frequently focus on the technical elements, paying insufficient attention to the social factors. *Leading Excellence* prioritizes the social aspect, highlighting its critical role in the overall system and providing leaders with an easy to follow handbook on developing flourishing people and organisations.

Skip Steward VP CIO Baptist Memorial Healthcare

As a West Point graduate and a former fighter pilot, I have been privileged to experience leadership in some of the most demanding and dynamic environments imaginable. These experiences have profoundly shaped my understanding of what it means to lead, influence, and achieve results, whether in the cockpit of a supersonic jet or within the structured yet fluid realms of Scrum and Scrum@Scale. Leadership, at its core, transcends the specifics of any field; it is about inspiring, guiding, and empowering others to surpass their limitations and achieve a common goal.

I highly recommend *Leading Excellence* to anyone committed to the pursuit of leadership excellence. It is a vital resource that promises not only to guide but also to inspire its readers to new heights of achievement. Explore its pages and find the inspiration to transform not just your approach to leadership, but your entire vision of what it means to lead.

Dr Jeff Sutherland Inventor and Co-Creator of Scrum and Scrum@Scale,Top Gun in the US Air Force, Former VP of Engineering and CTO or CEO of eleven software companies

Leading Excellence stands out vs. many other leadership books I have read due to how practical it is. From the authentic case studies to the exercises in the book, the real-world experience of the authors ooze into the words of this book.

The prose is not pretentious, the book is easy to read and follow and accessible for both the emerging leader, through to the c-suite. I recommend you not only read this book but also buy it as a gift for any of your team members that have leadership aspirations.

Anthony Vella Chief Transformation Officer, McMillan Shakespeare

I can't recommend this book highly enough, for leaders of any level of experience. *Leading Excellence* succeeds where other leadership books too often fall short, by remembering that the readers operate in a real world context. It provides a perfect blend of theory and real world practical application through highly relevant and engaging real world experiences. The book enables readers to bring theory to life in simple language that will help any leader in their journey. The book also reminds us that it is culture that sits at the heart of any organisation's success.

Andy Weir, BA, BSc, MBA, GAICD, Group Chief Technology & Transformation Officer, People First Bank, Advisory Board Member ABN Group Ltd

Leading Excellence

LEADING EXCELLENCE

5 Hats of the Adaptive Leader

2nd Edition

Chris Butterworth, Stephen Dargan and Brad Jeavons

Published by Chris Butterworth, Stephen Dargan and Brad Jeavons

First published in 2024 in Australia

2nd print run

Cover design and illustrations by Sandie Butterworth

Typeset by BookPOD

ISBN: 978-1-7636638-0-0 (paperback)
ISBN: 978-1-7636638-1-7 (ebook)

NATIONAL LIBRARY OF AUSTRALIA

A catalogue record for this book is available from the National Library of Australia

CONTENTS

WHY READ THIS BOOK?

This book will appeal to both established and aspiring leaders in every type of organisation. As leaders, we have a profound impact on the lives of the people we serve. Do you want to create a legacy that positively impacts your people, customers, and your communities?

This book explains the why and how of creating successful organisations with amazing cultures where people flourish.

As senior leaders working for many years all over the world, we came to realise we were often overwhelmed by the sheer size and complexity of what was expected of us. Today's leaders are faced with ever greater challenges, with a continuing acceleration of volatility, uncertainty, complexity, and ambiguity. As Canadian Prime Minister Justin Trudeau stated at the World Economic Forum in Davos in 2018, 'The pace of change has never been this fast, yet it will never be this slow again.'

For example, we are only just starting to understand some of the implications for the workplace of Artificial Intelligence. We also see additional pressure on leaders around environmental sustainability, psychological safety, and work-life balance.

So, the job is getting more difficult, more time consuming, and more pressurised than it ever has been before. We need to pause and reflect on how leaders can best serve their people, themselves, and their organisations. We need to cast a leader shadow that creates an amazing place to work whilst delivering sustainable, profitable growth.

We have been very fortunate to work with and for some fantastic leaders over the years, but the experience has been very mixed. We wanted to understand how we can all become fantastic leaders and provide a practical how-to guide to achieve this.

We will explain how to understand and manage your core belief system, how to build simple habits that will make you a more effective leader, and how to create a culture where you, your people, and your organisation can flourish.

It is a practical leadership handbook that provides an easy-to-follow approach to build the habits of an adaptive leader. It is full of real-life stories from around the world that every leader can relate to, and contains insights and tips based on the authors' many years of experience in senior leadership roles.

A key insight is the need for leaders to recognise that one size does not fit all in the way they lead their organisation and interact with their people. Leaders need to be adaptive to the context and the person.

To enable this, the authors have developed the concept of the 5 Hats of the Adaptive Leader. These enable leaders to understand why, when, and how to adapt their style appropriately in any given context.

It is an inspirational and motivational read that enables the reader to immediately take action to make a positive impact on themselves, their people, and their organisation.

CONTENTS BY CHAPTER

Chapter 1 Adaptive Leaders

Engaging all employees to improve and innovate towards an aligned vision and goals creates high-performance organisations. Leaders' behaviours play a large part in determining an organisation's engagement level. Leaders need to challenge themselves, asking if their behaviours are serving themselves, their own emotions or the growth of others?

Improving the ability to be an Adaptive Leader is the key to creating an engaged, high-performance culture and organisation. The most critical behaviour of an Adaptive Leader is pausing, thinking about the person and context surrounding them and responding with the ideal behaviour to help them grow. Building a habit loop to support this is essential.

Case Studies from BHP and Priestley's Gourmet Delights

Practical exercise: self-assessment and reflection.

Chapter 2 The Five Hats of the Adaptive Leader

The greatest leaders in our world in any organisation are constant learners and adaptive.

The adaptive leader's five hats of primary learning and skill development are Inspire, Teach, Support, Coach and Direct. Each hat is explored in detail with multiple examples.

Case Studies from Mauro Neves CEO Incitec Pivot.

Practical exercise: Current state self-assessment on applying The 5 Hats of the Adaptive Leader.

Chapter 3 Core Belief System

We all have a core belief system that drives our emotions. Understanding this can help us effectively control our emotions, stay in a place of thought, and be adaptive leaders. Understanding other people's core belief systems can help us to understand them more deeply. This knowledge helps us to adapt our approach and guide them towards their full potential. It is our behaviours and how we make people feel through these that define us as leaders. Defining ideal behaviours as a team/organisation provides us with a guiding light to be adaptive to improve ourselves and others.

Case Studies from Packaging, Agriculture, Wayne Bennett Super Coach

Practical exercise: Exploring your Core Belief System.

Chapter 4 Values – Respect, Humility and Trust

Respect, Humility and Trust are essential foundations for *Leading Excellence*.

We need to be clear on the behaviours that are expected in our organisation that demonstrate respect, humility and trust. Leaders need to lead by example in demonstrating these behaviours and constantly manage and reinforce them through recognition.

Case Studies from multiple sectors including financial services, pharmaceutical, steel processing.

Practical exercise: Defining ideal behaviours and what hats to wear to help embed them.

Chapter 5 Personal Purpose – Planting trees you may never sit under the shade of

Identify waste in your processes and coach your teams to use problem-solving tools to help remove failure demand so we focus more on what your customers value. Failure demand v real demand. Focus your teams on recruiting for ideal behaviours and character over technical ability. Leaders as teachers. Spend some personal time reflecting on what your 'legacy' will be as a leader. What do you want to be remembered for?

Case Studies from financial services.

Practical exercise: Practicing Look, Listen and Learn with a colleague.

Chapter 6 Personal Purpose – Nurturing the trees

Take time to understand each team member's purpose. Their 'why' they come to work each day. Use the different leadership hats to help them connect their purpose and how they contribute to the overall organisations purpose. See the true potential in every team member and create strong development pathways or systems to enable them to reach their potential. The Aspiring Leaders Assessment Matrix and Aspiring Leaders Development System.

Case Studies from financial services

Practical exercises: Understand your core purpose, understand some of your team's core belief system and practice using the Talent Assessment Matrix.

Chapter 7 Organisation Purpose – Rowing the boat together

To connect your people to the overall company's purpose requires leaders to get 'boring' in connecting their people to the overall company's purpose and vision. This requires reinforcement and repetition every day, everywhere, and with everybody. Alignment from the company CEO through to the frontline operator requires strong leadership and communications systems. Leaders need to work across the value stream and become 'enterprise leaders' to drive better outcomes for the organisation as a whole. How to use a Value Driver Tree.

Case Studies from financial services

Practical exercises: Creating a Customer Value Proposition, creating a team recognition routine linked to customer service.

Chapter 8 Ensure the Flower is blooming

Peoples' behaviours are always driven by something going on in their environment. The High Performance Formula. It's the role of the leader to truly understand every individual's intrinsic and extrinsic interference and 'dance with it'. If you want change to be sustainable, you must enable and empower your teams to lead the change. Have the courage to be vulnerable. Those leaders that do, connect more with their people.

Case Studies from financial services and mining.

Practical exercises: Identifying and understanding Interferences and 'dancing with them'.

Chapter 9 Listen to understand - two ears, one mouth

How to deliberately plan your time to focus on managing the culture you want. *Look, Listen, Learn* activities are a process of discovery - have an open mind and maintain curiosity throughout. It is never about validating preconceptions but rather discovering what is going on. Being a coaching leader is key to developing your people and freeing up your time.

Case Studies from food services, packaging, charity.

Practical exercises: Work out how much time you typically spend managing culture and develop a plan to increase it.

Chapter 10 Purpose and Systems drive behaviour

Define the behaviours you want to see to deliver your goals and ensure your systems are designed to support these behaviours. Ensure Freedom Within a Framework. Manage behaviours and systems with Key Behavioural Indicators and apply the Plan Do Check Act cycle to continuously improve the processes and behaviours.

Case Studies from food manufacturing and retailing

Practical exercises: Define some key behaviours needed to achieve your goals and experiment with some potential Key Behavioural Indicators to measure them.

Chapter 11 Summary and self-assessment exercises

Self-assessment exercises that help you understand the current state, and where you want to be and build a plan to close any gaps.

ACKNOWLEDGMENTS AND THANKS

To our contributors

Xanny Christophersen

Catherine Clark

Warren Cotter

Ron Gibson

Mauro Neves

James Olsen

Indrajit Ray and Patrizia Rando

Lawry Scandar

Gary Steele

Rob Telford

Dr Mark Williams

To our reviewers

Nadine Brennan

Nathan Charles

Mark Deluzio

Ben Dyson

Alex Hamilton

Pádraig Harrington

Andy Hecke

Peter Hines

Michael Hoseus

Tony Howarth

James Poulsen

Justin Scanlan

Skip Steward

Anthony Vella

Russell Warner

Andy Weir

To our amazing team

Sandie Butterworth - Kreative Nomad graphic designer

Nicole Gallant – Editor

Emily Jeavons – website creator

ABOUT THE AUTHORS

CHRIS BUTTERWORTH is a multi-award-winning author, international speaker, and coach. He is a certified Shingo Institute Academy Member, Faculty Fellow, master trainer, and examiner. He coaches executive teams and transfers continuous improvement knowledge across all levels of an organisation. Chris is a winner of the Best New Speaker of the Year Award for The Executive Connection (TEC) for his talk on *Lean Thinking*. He is the co-author of the three widely acclaimed Shingo publication-award-winning books: *4+1: Embedding a culture of continuous improvement, The essence of excellence—Creating a culture of continuous improvement* and *Why bother—Why and how to assess your continuous improvement culture*. He is also co-author of the book *Why care? How thriving individuals create thriving organisations* and the editor of the Shingo Institute book *Enterprise alignment and results*.

STEPHEN DARGAN A diverse and inclusive, customer-centric, driven, transformational leader with over 20 years of leadership experience spanning Australia and Europe. Stephen is a Shingo Institute Alumni, Shingo Facilitator Candidate and Examiner Candidate. Stephen is also a graduate of the Australian Institute of Company Directors and is a qualified Lean Six Sigma Black Belt through Cardiff University. Stephen has a strong track

record in transforming business cultures that drive sustainable growth and customer experiences. The strong principle-based strategies he deploys enable businesses to create systems that ultimately drive ideal behaviours and outcomes for customers, stakeholders, and shareholders. Stephen has built, developed, and led high-performing teams across financial services; retail, business, and commercial banking; asset finance; and, more recently, the mining industry.

BRAD JEAVONS is a facilitator and coach who helps organisations create cultures of continuous improvement and innovation towards their goals and who and what they serve. Brad's purpose is to help organisations create a better future economically, socially, and environmentally for future generations. Brad is the host of the Enterprise Excellence Podcast and Community. Brad is the author of the book *Agile sales, delivering customer journeys of value and delight*. Brad is a certified trainer and coach with the Lean Competency System (LCS) and the Agile Education Program. Brad is uniquely capable at facilitating and coaching individuals and teams at all levels of an organisation to help them define their path and improvement approaches, creating empowerment, energy, and commitment to achieving sustainable growth and performance.

FOREWORD

I have always been captivated by human behaviour. Growing up in a small country town in Australia during the 1970s and 1980s, I witnessed firsthand the powerful influence of human connection within a community. The positive and negative impacts of what Chris, Stephen, and Brad define as a group's Core Belief System, or culture, were evident all around me.

As a cognitive neuroscientist, my career has been dedicated to studying the brain. This journey has spanned 25 years and culminated in my writing 'The Connected Species.' It was with great pleasure that I read *Leading Excellence* a book designed to help leaders understand their critical role in fostering 'Connected' organisational cultures that benefit people, society, and the planet. The authors delve into creating a culture of continuous improvement and innovation, involving and engaging all levels of an organisation.

The authors explain with clarity why fostering an engaged culture of continuous improvement and innovation is vital. More engagement leads to a better culture, which in turn fosters greater agility and innovation, resulting in better outcomes for everyone. They also provide a straightforward yet challenging roadmap to achieve this transformation.

Humans thrive on connection. Historically, being part of a community was essential for survival, and exclusion often meant dire consequences.

I was fortunate to attend an early presentation by Dr. Giacomo Rizzolatti, who, along with his team, discovered mirror neurons—parts of our brain that interpret body language, facilitate empathy, and are crucial for social learning and understanding group dynamics.

Leaders, both formal and informal, have a profound impact on the culture of their teams and organisations. They wield social influence and authority, setting the tone through their actions and the way they make others feel. As Super Coach Wayne Bennett, featured in this book, asserts: 'Talk is cheap; it is what people see you do and how you make them feel that counts.' Leaders can shape culture positively through their behaviour or negatively by ignoring issues, impacting the entire organisation's culture.

Chris Butterworth, Stephen Dargan, and Brad Jeavons have researched and observed the effects of leadership on team cultures across thousands of organisations worldwide. Their extensive experience in organisational transformation has given them insights into both exemplary and poor leadership behaviours. Using their research, they define how leaders can create cultures of excellence by understanding core beliefs, values, and principles, and by using this knowledge to control their emotions and behaviours to serve others' growth.

Contributing to the development of their Core Belief System model, alongside organisational psychologist Lawry Scandar, was a privilege. This model is central to understanding both individual and organisational culture. A leader's ability to adapt and adjust behaviour according to the context and individuals they engage with requires a high level of self-awareness.

In cognitive neuroscience, we often liken the conscious and unconscious mind to a person riding an elephant. The rider represents the conscious brain, while the elephant symbolises the subconscious. A skilled rider understands and guides the elephant, leading to ideal behaviours, while an unskilled rider lets the elephant roam unchecked, driven by habit. *Leading Excellence* helps leaders understand their subconscious mind and consciously choose behaviours that foster growth and development in others.

The authors identify five key behaviours and skills, termed the five hats of the adaptive leader, essential for developing engaged cultures of excellence. These concepts are richly illustrated with case studies from successful leaders in various fields. Understanding and improving leadership behaviours is crucial because it is through behaviour that people learn and define organisational culture—not through posters or words alone, especially when actions do not align with rhetoric.

Leading Excellence provides leaders with proven strategies to define and cultivate culture across organisations, big and small. By *Leading Excellence*, you can transform your organisation into a motivated, continuously improving, and innovative culture at every level. Organisations, like a herd of people riding elephants, achieve greatness when aligned with their Core Belief System and guided by conscious, ideal behaviours.

This book is essential reading for current and aspiring leaders who aim to serve and achieve great outcomes for their people, themselves, and the greater good. Enjoy your journey through this book and in your continuous efforts to connect with your people and lead excellence.

Sincerely,
Mark A. Williams, PhD
Professor of Cognitive Neuroscience
Director of Rethinking the Brain

1

ADAPTIVE LEADERS

We are constantly amazed at the results organisations achieve when they engage more employees to innovate and align toward a shared purpose and goals. I've seen customer and employee satisfaction double, year-on-year growth and profitability improve by over 20%, and productivity multiply tenfold (Sutherland, 2019).

Yet, most organisations are only performing 'OK', some profit, some growth, but struggle to hire and retain great people, hit ambitious growth rates, or, for not-for-profits, break even. Leaders work tirelessly, juggling challenges to maintain customer service and prevent burnout for both themselves and their teams.

Here's the reality: in low-engagement organisations, all problems funnel to middle and senior leaders. These leaders juggle daily tasks, crises,

1

and strategic projects, but the weight is unsustainable. They burn out, disengage, and lose satisfaction as projects fail.

Meanwhile, frontline employees feel unheard. Leaders, overwhelmed, can't solve raised issues or communicate effectively, leaving employees to think, What's the point of speaking up if nothing changes?

The real danger? These organisations lack the agility to navigate rapid challenges and seize opportunities in a fast-moving world. High-performing organisations, those primed to respond effectively, have high engagement, strong capabilities, and clear alignment.

The global data highlights the gap: just 23% of the workforce is actively engaged (Gallup, 2023). So, where does your organisation stand?

The issue is clear: leadership drives engagement. Gallup tells us that a direct leader accounts for 70% of team engagement. At its core, leadership comes down to behaviour. An employee's entire experience of a leader is shaped by what they say, how they say it, their actions, and body language.

> We need to ask ourselves a critical question: Who are we serving, ourselves or our people?

We have found two additional engagement killers: employees lacking clear, meaningful goals (linked to purpose) and the autonomy to contribute towards them. This is prevalent particularly with front line employees. It's like a sporting team where players enter the field without knowing where the goals are, seeing no scoreboard, and feeling powerless to improve. Coaches stressed and overwhelmed sit in the box trying to solve every problem while scrambling to fix a game plan they can't effectively implement. Who would want to play, or watch that game?

But imagine the potential. What if we engaged all players, freed up coaches (leaders), developed their skills to lead with ideal behaviours, build their capability to train and support team development, align purpose and goals, support the team to create a transparent scoreboard, and define the field of play? That team would dominate, especially if the competition remained disengaged and aimless.

The secret to success is simple: improve leadership behaviour. As leaders, we need to ask ourselves a critical question: Who are we serving, ourselves or our people?

LEADERS WHO SERVE— ENGAGING EVERY HEART, MIND, AND BODY

The idea of leaders who serve (Sutherland, 2020) isn't new, it's been around for years. But the way it's often interpreted creates problems. Many see it as leaders fully subordinating themselves to employees: solving every problem, constantly helping, and sharing knowledge at every turn.

This interpretation reinforces two leadership behaviours that, when overused, drive employee disengagement (see Figure 1.1).

FIGURE 1.1: Overused leadership belief and behaviour.

When I see leaders who care deeply, want to serve, and constantly help their teams, I notice a common trap: they can overuse these behaviours. Instead of empowering their teams, they create a sense of inadequacy, team members feel incapable of solving problems or making a difference. I call this leadership behaviour the ultimate carer.

On the other extreme is the know-it-all. These leaders were often promoted because they excelled in their previous roles. They think the best way to serve their team is by constantly sharing their knowledge, telling team members exactly what to do or overwhelming them with a flood of ideas. The result? Chaos, confusion, and a lack of focus.

Both behaviours, being the ultimate carer or know-it-all, serve the leader's emotions more than the team's needs. We overuse these habits because they feel good. Helping someone or sharing knowledge gives us a dopamine hit, a quick dose of pleasure that reinforces the behaviour.

Thanks to Charles Duhigg (2014) and others, we understand how habits form and become deeply ingrained (see Figure 1.2).

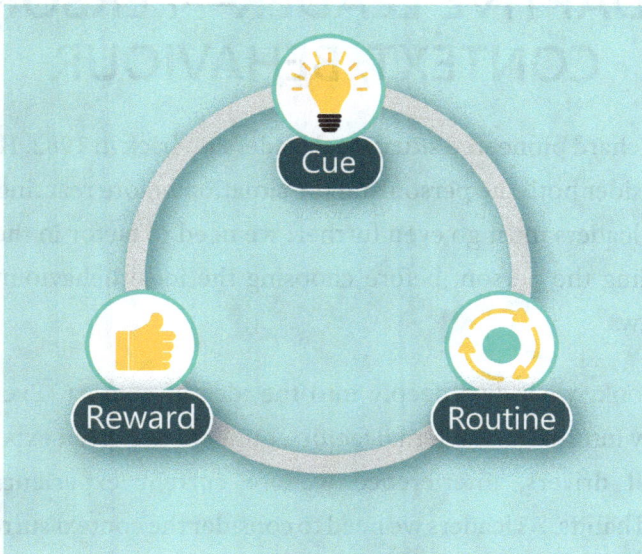

FIGURE 1.2: Habit Loop.

Habits form simply: a trigger happens, like an employee asking us a question, we jump in with an answer, and we get our reward: that quick dopamine hit for feeling helpful or knowledgeable.

But leaders who truly serve act differently. They focus on what will best support the growth of the other person in that moment. This approach helps every team member develop their capacity and move closer to their full potential. It creates a learning culture, where people grow, improve, and innovate daily, boosting engagement, agility, customer satisfaction, and results.

To do this, we need to choose our behaviours intentionally, serving others instead of seeking emotional rewards for ourselves. Ultimately, leaders who serve are skilled adaptive leaders.

ADAPTIVE LEADER—PERSON, CONTEXT, BEHAVIOUR

Ken Blanchard pioneered situational leadership back in 1982. He taught us to consider both the person and the situation before reacting. Today, I believe leaders must go even further: we need to factor in the *context* surrounding the person, before choosing the ideal behaviour to help them grow.

In this book, we'll dive deeply into the idea of context. Everyone is shaped by internal and external factors, our genetics, lived experiences, emotional drivers, interference we are current experiencing and ingrained habits. As leaders we need to consider the context surrounding people we serve and adapt to get the best out of them.

As leaders, we rely on behaviours that have worked for us before, our 'go-to' responses. We've seen these behaviours succeed, so they become habits reinforced by the reward of positive results. But how often do we truly choose behaviours that help the other person grow?

The good news is this: to become more adaptive, leaders only need to enhance one core skill, pause......think....... respond (see Figure 1.3).

FIGURE 1.3: Adaptive Leader.

When someone engages with us, we are triggered, feel the urge to react based on natural habits. An adaptive leader does not react, they pause, consider the person and the context surrounding them, before choosing their behaviour to help them grow.

Context varies greatly. We need to ask ourselves: What do I know about this person? What emotional challenges are they facing, at work or in their personal life? What other forces could be influencing their current attitude or behaviour? By linking what we know about the person, the context, and the situation, we can respond in a way that serves their growth, not our own emotions. Traditional management told us to leave personal life at the door. But that's not realistic. Emotions and challenges don't vanish, we might suppress them, but they still affect us.

We're in an era of respect, honouring backgrounds, beliefs, and preferences. Understanding context is at the heart of serving others and adapting our behaviour to support their growth. In Chapter 8, we'll explore this concept further with case studies and introduce the high-performance formula.

The behaviour of pausing, considering the person and context, and then responding sounds simple, but it's far from easy. As a leader, we need to be conscious of our emotional response, catch ourselves before reacting, and take a breath. Slowing down, even momentarily, allows us to think carefully about the person and context, and respond in a way that serves the other person.

For many of us, this requires a conscious change in habit. While we might adapt well at times, how often do we truly practise this? By improving our ability to adapt, we can better serve others, helping them grow toward their full potential instead of being driven by our own emotions.

The first step to improving anything is having a reason to do it. Without emotional investment or a strong 'why,' meaningful change rarely happens. Changing habits is hard work, but it's the key to becoming a leader who truly serves.

DEVELOPING IDEAL BEHAVIOUR

The idea that new habits can be formed in 21 days is a myth. Forming habits depends on several factors: How difficult is the new habit? How ingrained is the old one? How strong and immediate is the reward? And most importantly, how powerful is our motivation or purpose for changing?

To replace an old habit, we need to repeat the new one enough times for it to become stronger. This isn't easy, which is why having a clear emotional driver, a bigger reason to change than to stay the same is so critical (see Figure 1.4: Leadership Motivation & Habit Change).

FIGURE 1.4: Leadership Motivation and Habit Change.

As an adaptive leader, our goal is to create an organisation where every person is engaged, learning, and growing toward their full potential and, in turn, the organisation's full potential.

The first step to becoming a more adaptive leader is understanding why I want to change. Why am I willing to put in the effort to pause, consider the person, the context surrounding them, and choose the ideal behaviour instead of falling back on old habits and reacting subconsciously?

Let's look at some examples of how pausing, thinking, and responding intentionally can make all the difference (see Table 1.1).

Pause, consider the person and context surrounding them, and choose the ideal behaviour.

9

TABLE 1.1: Examples of person, context, and ideal behaviour.

Person	Context	Ideal Behaviour
All people.	Safety situation.	Direct the person to stop, get out of the way, etc.
New employee, low level of skill and competence, highly engaged and motivated.	Has a question on how to perform a task. You know they are anxious as they are in a new role. They are also facing some challenges at home with one of their children's health.	Ask them how they are feeling, actively listen, and show empathy to their response. Ask them if they would like you to take them through some training on the process?
Long term employee, highly skilled, proud of their capability and job they do.	The employee has achieved poor results this month. You know they are struggling with a recent relationship breakup.	Support them by showing empathy and actively listening to their responses. Move into coaching once you have established a foundation of trust and calmer emotions.

There are countless examples we could explore, and I'm sure you've already thought of some from your own experience. That's why I encourage you to first define your why, your core motivator or emotional driver to improve as an adaptive leader who serves the growth of others and then use the rest of this book to build your knowledge and skills.

As we've seen in this chapter, being an adaptive leader means pausing, considering the person, the context surrounding them, and choosing behaviours that help others grow.

There have been a lot of documented teachings on Adaptive Leadership, most notably the wonderful work by Ronald Heifetz and Marty Linsky 'The Practice of Adaptive Leadership'. Their book is a foundational resource, offering strategies for leaders to improve performance, navigate uncertainty, and embrace emotional intelligence, feedback, and experimentation.

This work focuses on leaders' ability to show emotional intelligence, lead fairly, develop themselves and experiment, be open to feedback, switch course if needed and focus on win-win problem solving. *Leading Excellence, The 5 hats of the Adaptive Leader* compliments Ronald and Marty's book well, we recommend their book for further reading.

CASE STUDY – ROB TELFORD & YANDI

I have been fortunate to be a contracting assessor for BHP on their excellence journey. BHP has an excellence program known as the BHP Operating System. It focuses on developing eighty thousand problem solvers and continuous improvers at BHP to help the organisation live its purpose of bringing people and resources together to build a better world.

I have assessed many sites, but what I saw at the Yandi Iron Ore site in the Pilbara of northern Western Australia was amazing. At Yandi, there are several cultural principles that are lived by everyone, from front-line employees to senior leadership:

- **It's the human moments that count.**

I heard stories of leaders who had flown down to a team member's family home to spend some time with them when the team member's wife was suffering badly from cancer.

- **We are all mates, have each other's back, and keep each other safe.**

Whenever I asked about safety and what it meant to team members, Yandi team members explained how they stayed conscientious in their work, watching each other every day. 'We are happy for each other to call us out if they see a process not being followed or anything slightly unsafe.'

- **The standard you walk past is the standard you accept.**

I observed maintenance workshops with big open doors looking out to the red dust of the Pilbara. I also observed clean surfaces on benches, toolboxes, and floors in these workshops. I opened toolbox drawers and cupboards and saw that everything was clean and in its place.

When asked how this was achieved, a front-line team member responded, 'The standard you walk past is the standard you accept. We all lead and sustain this standard because our work environment impacts our behaviour, and we are focused on keeping each other safe.'

During the assessment, I was unable to understand how the site had developed this culture: the leaders who had implemented the change many years ago were no longer at the site, yet everyone still lived the behaviours that sustained the culture.

A month later, I was still thinking about what I saw at Yandi, when I conducted another BHP Operating System Assessment on the east coast of Australia at Daunia. I partnered with another BOS assessor, Daniel Horner, someone who has worked with BHP for many years and is truly passionate about helping improve culture to create better outcomes.

While walking between team member interviews at Daunia, I opened up to Dan about what I had seen at Yandi. Dan stopped walking, looked at me and said, 'I worked at Yandi around the time that cultural journey started.' He said you needed to talk to Rob Telford, who led the Yandi site at that time.

I was lucky enough to track Rob down and setup a time to record a Podcast with him for the Enterprise Excellence Podcast. What is to follow covers the story of Rob Telford and the Yandi site. The adaptive leader behaviours he and his team used to truly serve others. At the time this book was being written, Rob was a Vice President at BHP. Rob had been in many roles over a lengthy career at BHP, starting as a front-line operator. Rob mentioned that when he became General Manager of Operations at Yandi, it was his first step into senior leadership of a site.

Very quickly, Rob and his team found themselves in a position where no leader wants to be: they had two fatalities on site. First Paul, and then Adam. Rob was at home when he got the call at midnight notifying him of Paul's accident and passing. The second fatality, Adam, occurred shortly after. Rob had just landed on a flight into the region; he was sitting in his hire car when he took the call.

Rob was shell-shocked. His initial thought was that this was too hard. He had just started as a senior leader of this site and they had lost two people on his watch. Rob thought, 'Who will it be who helps to turn this around if it is not me?' Rob's thinking changed in that hire car from 'this was too much' to a fierce determination that 'we need to get the culture at Yandi to a better place so that this does not happen again.' Rob thought, 'Enough is enough; we will make Yandi a great place to work.'

Rob met with one of the emergency response coordinators for the site at the airport, who offered to drive him to Yandi. Halfway to the site, Rob demonstrated the first example of being an adaptive leader: he asked if they could pull over so he could collect his thoughts and consider how he would show up for the team at Yandi and demonstrate ideal behaviour.

Rob walked around in the red dirt at the side of the road, thinking about the people working at the site and the context of what had occurred. Rob knew that how he presented that day would make a big contribution towards winning the support he needed to improve the site for the future.

Rob quickly demonstrated a second example of being an adaptive leader: he engaged with his leadership team and worked with them to clearly define their purpose moving forward, the right of everyone to get home safely.

He firstly aligned with the leadership team and the rest of the site on this common purpose. Rob believes that the person who most knows how to improve something and make it safer is the person doing the work 12 hours a day. Rob and his leadership team engaged with the front-line teams, working with them to understand where they were at and truly understand what was going on.

Rob and his team, through this approach, found Rob's belief to be true. Through the weeks and months of walking the site and listening actively, they learned about the risks and what needed to be done to move forward to being a safer site.

Throughout the process, Rob realised the importance of really listening and that it was something we are not taught at school. Listening is a crucial skill for being an adaptive leader. Truly understanding a person and the context surrounding them requires asking open questions and listening intently, showing empathy to responses, and asking further why and what questions to go deeper. The adaptive leader approach by Rob and his team helped them to learn about the risks and challenges faced by the team.

During this time, Rob had several team members come to him who were angry and upset. Rob knew that these people, who could be viewed as being against him, were his greatest allies; they just hadn't become one yet. They are people who care and have energy for the cause you are working on and the purpose and vision you are chasing.

Rob found great allies in these early days, such as Tom Dorion and many others whom Rob and his team sat down with and listened to, learnt from, and provided resources and space to help him move forward and improve. Rob believes that people usually care in the workplace. It is the way our behaviour as leaders brings out their voices, together with the systems and processes we have in place to enable this, that counts.

Rob and his team demonstrated adaptive leader skills with each person they met, listening intently, considering the person and the context surrounding them, and then choosing their behaviour to help the person while showing respect and learning themselves.

Yandi started making real progress towards a safer workplace. Improvements in processes and culture at all levels of the organisation was enabling the site to move forward towards a safe, performing site, a great place to work. Rob and his leadership team sustained an approach of leading from the front to stay connected, listen, and learn. Rob and his team focused on culture change and improvement through thousands of conversations in the field, leading to thousands of micro decisions and improvements that always put the person first.

Their absolute focus on the goal established at the start of this journey provided a super clear focus for conversations and improvement efforts. The priority was getting everyone home at the end of a shift without even a scratch. A groundswell of energy and language was building, and that was the start of the cultural principles our author heard during his assessment at Yandi over ten years later.

Rob and his leadership team's behaviour played a large part in gaining support from more team members and sustaining the journey. One team member spoke to Rob one day, saying, 'I now know you are serious about this journey, and this is not just a short-term thing.'

There was a policy at the mining camp that people followed the footpaths and did not cut across corners, particularly across roads. One night, this team member saw Rob pull up at the site late and follow the footpaths rather than save time and cut across the road, even though it was quiet and Rob would have assumed no one was looking. This was the turning point for that team member to realise that Rob meant what he said and was in on the journey.

The third adaptive leader moment of Rob being a leader who serves came when he was being driven down to a shift-change meeting by a superintendent. They were cutting it fine for the meeting start and the superintendent drove across an intersection, resulting in a large oncoming truck having to brake and slow down. Rob thought of the person (his superintendent) and the context (safety) and straightaway had a direct conversation with the superintendent about what had just occurred: a near miss.

When Rob arrived at the shift control room, he observed several signs from the people there that they had lost their focus on the ideal behaviours necessary to ensure that everyone gets home safe. Again, Rob thought of the people (they were not clear on what they needed to do to prioritise safety) and the context (they were slipping).

Rob told everyone in the shift control room and his superintendent that the whole mine would be shut down immediately and that they would gather at the mining camp.

This was a big call by Rob; at the time, Yandi was the largest iron ore mine in the world, with the iron ore pricing sitting at $200/tonne.

Everyone congregated back at the mining camp; there were well over 600 people on the grass. Rob stood to the side for a moment, reflecting on what he observed that morning and the past few weeks. He thought about the leadership behaviours they were and were not exuding recently. Rob then walked to the front of the gathering. The first thing he did was apologise to everyone. He acknowledged that they had been leading the site incorrectly, which was not OK. Rob said that that was on him. He assured everyone that the leadership team would collaborate and realign the mine's safety practices reinforcing the goal of everyone getting home safely.

Rob sent his leadership team out to their workplaces to look at them through the lens of safety and culture. He told them not to return to him until they felt that they had confirmed their ideal behaviours and that their respective work areas were ready to operate safely, however long it took. The entire site did not run again for nearly two days.

The adaptive leader approach–where Rob demonstrated that he was thinking about the people and the context surrounding them and purposely chose ideal behaviours to help them grow and move towards their full potential, truly worked. Any critic in the team who still did not believe that leadership were truly serious about implementing a change in organisational culture, was now on board.

As an adaptive leader, Rob believes that taking off down a strategic/change road and looking back at people, shouting and jumping up and down to hurry them along is counterproductive. You need to go back to where they are, understand them and the context surrounding them, and adapt your behaviour to help them move along the road with you. This is truly the essence of an adapting leader who serves.

Rob, his team, and subsequent team members continue to lead Yandi to sustain and improve their culture and performance up to the point when our author arrived at the site over ten years later. Yandi now has an amazing safety record. In addition to this, as you leave the site you see the boot tree, where team members leaving Yandi hang up their boots to leave a little bit of themselves behind.

Yandi also became the site within BHP renowned for quickly producing additional tons of iron ore when needed. Its productivity and agility have made it the site that other BHP sites and operations speak about. Rob Telford and his team have truly demonstrated how to be adaptive leaders. They focused on being leaders who served the safety and growth of every team member at Yandi.

CASE STUDY: XANNY CHRISTOPHERSEN & PRIESTLEY'S GOURMET DELIGHTS

I was fortunate to get to know a young leader called Xanny Christophersen. Xanny has held many leadership roles at Priestley's Gourmet Delights, Australia's largest high-quality sweet and savoury dessert manufacturer. Over many years, she has worked to evolve her habits and skills as a leader to truly became a leader who serves.

Xanny started her career at Priestley's in the field with customers and then on the factory floor. When Xanny first moved into a leadership role, she was only 25. At that time, the organisation needed more developmental support for new leaders. Xanny worked with what existing leadership skills and habits she had in those early times but like many young leaders thrown into senior positions early in their careers, there was some needed improvement. Xanny had the tendency to give orders rather than seek to understand. Driving her team hard towards results, often leaving them behind rather than explaining the 'why' and bringing them on the journey.

Xanny was a great networker and linked with some good people who helped her grow as a leader, such as John Broadbent, Earl Roberts, Brad Jeavons and others. Xanny fostered a mindset of humility, openness, and growth. She became a constant learner, seeking knowledge and advice wherever she could. Throughout this journey, Xanny grew to know the concept of leaders who serve: being a leader who serves the growth of others around them rather than their own emotions and ambitions.

Xanny grew her self-awareness and the ability to seek to understand others and truly understand the people she leads and works with. Xanny developed humble leadership, knowing that she does not have to have all the answers and leaned into the knowledge of the team around her. In doing so, she engaged with them, built their capability, and achieved greater results.

Xanny has constantly improved her ability to pause rather than react and to consider the person and context surrounding the individual, which enables her to choose her behaviour to help their growth.

Xanny and her team established an organisational purpose: 'Simply Creating Happiness,' creating simplicity and happiness for customers, team members, and the planet. This purpose has helped Xanny and her team to lead the change in behaviour of everyone within the organisation by focusing on the growth of all personnel, accepting and using the previous experience of others, and reducing their footprint on the planet.

After years of development and honing her leadership skills, Xanny has rightfully earned her role as the CEO of Priestley's. As CEO she values the culture of 365-degree feedback, support and development the organisation has available to its staff. She values the team she has around her, who now believe in the organisation's purpose and provide her with as much input and growth support as she gives to them.

The path forward for Xanny is one of ongoing personal development. She is passionate about the organisations and her own growth to improve how the people serve the planet and the growth of others and, in doing so, simply creating happiness.

These case studies also demonstrate the many different ideal behaviour hats an Adaptive Leader can wear, depending on the person/people and context surrounding them. We are going to explore these hats in depth in the next chapter.

KEY TAKEAWAYS TO PUT INTO PRACTICE THAT WILL DRIVE A HIGH PERFORMING, ENGAGED CULTURE

1. Engaging all employees to improve and innovate towards an aligned vision, purpose and goals creates high-performance organisations.

2. Leadership behaviours play a large part in an organisation's engagement level. Are our behaviours serving ourselves, our own emotions, or the growth of others?

3. Improving our ability to be an adaptive leader is key to creating an engaged, high-performance culture and organisation. The most critical behaviour of an adaptive leader is pausing, thinking about the person and context surrounding them, and then responding with the ideal behaviour to help them grow.

ACTIVITY 1

Use table 1.2 below to reflect on your leadership behaviours over the past few days. Consider people and context where you have slipped into the area of 'Ultimate Carer' or 'Know it All' leader. In the thoughts to improve column note how you could have approach each one differently to more effectively help the other person grow.

TABLE 1.2: Activity 1.

Ultimate Carer	Know it All	Thoughts to improve

2

THE FIVE HATS OF THE ADAPTIVE LEADER

As a leader, continual learning is key to navigating current and future challenges (Collison, 2017). It's logical, leaders who constantly improve are better equipped to develop the skills and behaviours needed for what's ahead.

However, the demands of leadership often feel overwhelming. Balancing daily pressures with the effort required to build new habits can feel impossible. So, what should we prioritise to optimise my learning and maximise impact?

With over 100 years of combined experience in organisational improvement, we, the authors of this book, have seen the same leadership challenges globally. To uncover the ideal behaviours of high-performing leaders, we drew on thousands of organisational excellence surveys, field observations and leadership coaching we have conducted.

From this research, we identified the critical behaviours and skills that outstanding leaders use to create engaged, high-performance cultures. By comparing these findings to poor leadership results, we pinpointed the five most critical behaviours leaders should focus on.

If we, as leaders, channel our efforts into mastering these behaviours, the potential to amplify employee engagement and performance is enormous (see Figure 2.1).

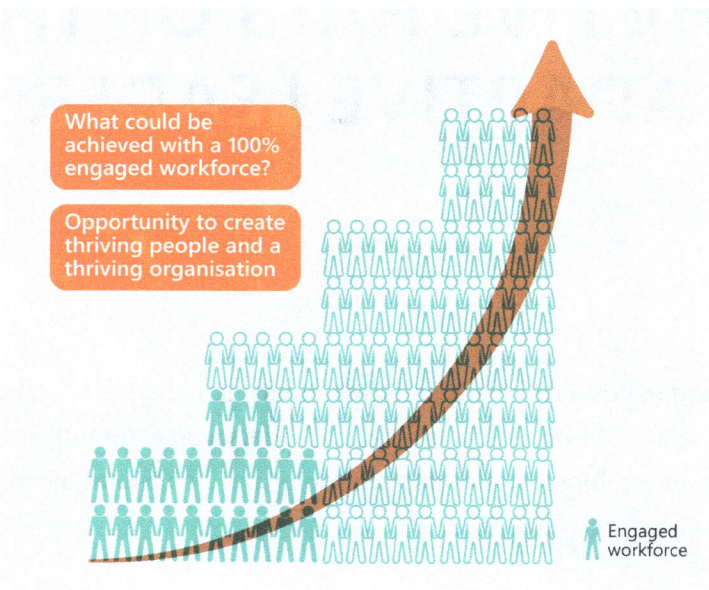

FIGURE 2.1: Global employee engagement opportunity (Gallup, 2023).

Through our research, we identified five ideal leadership behaviours that adaptive leaders use to serve their people, foster growth, and achieve extraordinary results. Adaptive leaders switch between these behaviours like wearing different hats, depending on the person and the context surrounding them.

The idea of 'hats' in leadership isn't new (Bono, 1985; Banoub, 2022; Taylor, 2019; Young, 2023), but it's a powerful framework for helping leaders adjust their approach to suit different individuals and situations.

The five hats of the adaptive leader that emerged from our research are outlined in Figure 2.2.

FIGURE 2.2: 5 Hats of the adaptive leader.

The 5 Hats of the adaptive leader are:

1. **Inspire**—Understand an individual's purpose and goals and align these to the organisation. Bring this understanding and alignment to life constantly.

2. **Teach**—Train an individual in an area of skill they do not currently possess to help them and their team to move towards their purpose, vision, and goals.

3. **Support**—Support people in transforming knowledge into competence. Support people in emotional times.

4. **Coach**—Coach an individual or team to enhance their skills and continuously move towards their own, their team's, and the organisation's purpose, vision, and goals.

5. **Direct**—Direct a person or group out of harm's way. Direct an individual or group when culture is being negatively impacted.

One of our greatest challenges as leaders is consciously pausing to consider the person and context surrounding them before choosing the right 'hat' to wear.

Another challenge lies in our ability to effectively wear these hats. Our skill level in inspiring, teaching, supporting, coaching, and directing determines the quality of every interaction. We all have strengths and weaknesses, there's no right or wrong, but the key is to continually improve the skills that help ourselves and others grow toward our full potential.

Without consistent growth in these five hats, we risk stagnation, or worse, regression, in our leadership capabilities. This can trigger a downward spiral, with our leadership shadow casting a diminishing impact on those we lead.

The good news? There are only five hats to focus on. By mastering these, we can strengthen our leadership shadow, drive better cultural and performance outcomes, and become a leader who truly serves the growth of others.

Let's dive into each of these behavioural hats, why they matter, when to wear them, what happens if we don't, and how to wear them well.

INSPIRE HAT

Without appropriate motivation and emotion, humans will not develop new habits (Duhigg, 2014). Furthermore, for individuals, teams, or entire organisations to grow, continuous learning, capability development, innovation, and improvement are essential. The greatest organisations have fostered strong cultures of continuous learning and improvement.

These facts highlight the importance of the inspire hat. The ability to inspire individuals and teams is a critical skill for adaptive leaders. It lays the foundation for an environment where people are motivated to learn and grow.

However, the inspire hat is one of the least worn by leaders, despite being vital to achieving excellence. Many leaders mistakenly believe they inspire their teams by constantly helping (the ultimate carer) or swooping in to solve problems (the know-it-all). While these behaviours may appear inspiring in films, they often disempower and demotivate employees in real life.

Leaders who fail to wear the inspire hat risk leading teams that lack motivation, stagnate, and fail to improve, contributing to the global employee engagement crisis. Without motivation and emotion, employees lack the drive to change and grow.

There are several core beliefs of leaders that create this undesirable culture, for example:

1. Employees are paid well and should simply do their job.
2. There's no time to sit with team members; things are fine as they are.

3. Motivation is unnecessary or 'fluffy.'

4. Team members lack the intelligence or capability to handle complexity.

The inspire hat is crucial for countering these issues. Research by Jim Collins in Good to Great (2001) underscores the importance of constancy of purpose. Collins found that great leaders consistently refer to purpose, bringing it to life daily to drive engagement, alignment, and energy. Purpose serves as the north star, essential for overcoming the challenges of habit change and sustaining organisational progress.

The most successful leaders and organisations wear the inspire hat consistently, embedding purpose in their daily interactions. Let's examine specific moments when adaptive leaders can don the inspire hat to engage and motivate their teams effectively in Table 2.1.

TABLE 2.1: Person and context—inspire hat.

Person	Context
Potential new ideal employee for the organisation.	This person is in a job interview, meeting with their potential new leader for the first time. They are motivated and engaged as they are keen to get the job.
A new employee who has a quieter personality and is process and data driven.	Just joined the team, currently in the onboarding phase. They are feeling nervous and excited. They know some initial information about the organisation and team's purpose, vision, and goals. As a leader, we know some initial information about them, but not their purpose, values, vision, and goals, either personally or at work.

Person	Context
An existing employee who is typically upbeat and energetic. They are social and highly talkative.	This employee is looking a bit flat; they have had a high workload recently and seem to be feeling tired and low on energy. You are unsure of other factors impacting them outside of work.
Long-term employee who is highly focused on others, a selfless person.	This person has been in the same role for five-plus years; they are asking about their future and what's next. We have not had this discussion for a long time.

The most effective way to wear the inspire hat is to think deeply about what you know about the person and the context surrounding them and then adapt your approach to wearing the inspire hat to align with their personality and who they are.

For example, a new employee with a quieter, process and data driven personality may benefit from a calm and structured introduction. The leader could say, 'We have a process for new employees that helps us understand each other and identify ways to work together to achieve your goals, the team's goals, and the organisation's goals.' This conversation allows the leader to explore the individual's career and personal goals, uncovering their purpose and aligning it with the team and organisation.

For a long-term employee, the leader may already understand some of their goals and aspirations. By paraphrasing their understanding during a one-on-one meeting, the leader can validate or refine this understanding, asking, 'How accurate is my understanding? Is there anything I've missed?'

Another valuable technique is directly asking team members, 'What do I do as your leader that fills your motivation bucket?' and 'What do I do that empties it?' (see Figure 2.3). These questions provide insights into how a leader's behaviours impact team motivation. Effective leadership behaviours can significantly raise or lower the level of motivation and inspiration within a team.

FIGURE 2.3: Motivation bucket filling and emptying behaviours.

Let's explore a real-life case study of how wearing the inspire hat as an adaptive leader can lead to excellent outcomes for everyone involved, an experience I had firsthand.

I was leading a mid-tier organisation and had just finalised the hire of a high-calibre graduate named Anthony. He came from a top school and university and a highly successful family with their own businesses. I was thrilled to have found someone of his calibre.

However, the managing director congratulated me on the hire with a caveat: he doubted we could retain Anthony long-term. 'We're too small,' he said, 'and there won't be enough opportunities for him to progress.'

That comment gave me pause. I knew the time and effort required to onboard and develop new team members effectively. After reflecting overnight, I decided to fully back Anthony and commit to supporting his growth throughout his employee journey.

I began by having a one-on-one meeting with Anthony, focused on understanding his personal and professional goals. I asked what motivated him to pursue these goals and probed deeper to uncover the emotional drivers behind them, his core purpose.

What I discovered was that Anthony was highly family oriented. Personally, he was focused on marrying his girlfriend, buying a home, and providing a good life for his future family, including sending his children to quality schools. Professionally, he wanted to progress to senior leadership, earn good money, and help his team grow and reach their full potential, all tied back to his purpose of supporting his family.

Our organisation's purpose was to help customers and employees achieve their goals, with a focus on growth for both the business and its people. I saw a clear alignment between Anthony's personal and professional purpose and the organisations. I knew that achieving the organisation's goals towards its purpose would create opportunities for Anthony to grow, fulfill his purpose, and achieve his goals.

Over the years, I worked closely with Anthony. While I undoubtedly made mistakes along the way, sometimes filling his motivation bucket and other times emptying it, we built a strong foundation of trust and psychological safety. We were always open to raising issues, seeking feedback, and learning from each other. Actively listening and acting on feedback solidified that trust, as we will explore in future chapters.

As of this writing, Anthony is now the Chief Executive Officer (CEO) of the organisation. He has a wonderful family, children attending top schools, and a fabulous home with his wife. While this might sound like a fairy tale, Anthony's journey was filled with ups and downs. The alignment of his personal and professional goals and purpose with the organisation's purpose, coupled with constant conversations, allowed us to maintain focus, even through tough times, and achieve excellent outcomes for Anthony, his family, and the organisation.

Like all five hats of the adaptive leader, the inspire hat is essential. Throughout this book, we will explore more ways to wear this hat effectively.

TEACH HAT

From an early age, people experience the teach hat, whether its parents teaching them to ride a bike, teachers instructing them in school, or leaders guiding them in their first job. Teaching experiences vary widely, with some inspiring growth and others hindering it. A learning culture within organisations has been shown to create excellent outcomes, yet fostering such a culture remains inconsistent, beginning with new employee onboarding.

When employees join a company, they start with 100% motivation and engagement. However, this engagement can decline rapidly, often influenced by the emotional and educational support they receive in their first weeks. Over the past few decades, there has been a shift toward outsourcing teaching or embedding it in software systems. Many new hires are subjected to long periods of online training rather than personal engagement with leaders and teammates.

This trend has led many leaders to delegate the teach hat to Learning and Development teams or external providers. While external training and software systems have their place, over-reliance on these methods risks deskilling and disempowering both leaders and employees. Leaders who are not directly involved in teaching lose ownership of their team's development.

Studies, including those by Hermann Ebbinghaus (1913), have shown that learning retention declines rapidly without reinforcement and practice. When leaders disengage from teaching, they also disengage from wearing the other adaptive leader hats, ongoing coaching and support needed to help an employee truly build competence. Employees often struggle in their roles, relying on peers for learning, sometimes with inaccurate or suboptimal outcomes. This lack of direct leadership in teaching can hinder the development of essential skills and capabilities.

Considering the critical role of continuous learning and growth in the success of adaptive organisations, the teach hat is indispensable (Sutherland, 2014). Adaptive leaders must evaluate the person and the context surrounding them before putting on the teach hat to support growth and development.

Let's explore examples of leaders effectively wearing this hat.

TABLE 2.2: Person and context—teach hat.

Person	Context
New employee.	It is their first day, they know little about the organisation, team, and processes.
Employee who has been with the organisation for a long time.	They have just moved to a new team. They have been involved in a quality issue; a process they know very little about.
Long term employee.	The employee is about to perform a process they have not been involved in previously. They are not motivated and are highly disengaged. You understand they are facing some challenges in their marriage currently.
Any employee.	The employee has defined a new goal for the future as part of their personal planning. They are motivated and inspired to progress themselves in this area.

To wear the teach hat effectively, an adaptive leader must pause and consider both the person and the context before reacting. Many workplace quality and safety issues stem from a lack of competence in team members, yet individuals are often blamed for problems they were never adequately trained to handle.

New employees typically show little resistance to training. A leader focused on their growth can establish an onboarding plan that starts intensively and gradually reduces over time. For longer-term employees, personal development or thriving plans (Warner et al., 2024) provide a framework for continuous learning, focusing on both psychological well-being and skill development to maximise growth and improvement.

Unfortunately, leaders are rarely taught how to teach effectively. Traditional lecturing methods, which many leaders have experienced (at Home, School or University), do not align well with adult learning principles. Adults value their past experiences and existing knowledge, and they need to be actively involved in the learning process rather than being lectured to.

One effective approach is the adult learning loop, which helps leaders improve how they use the teach, support, and coach hats to enhance their team's capabilities (see Figure 2.4).

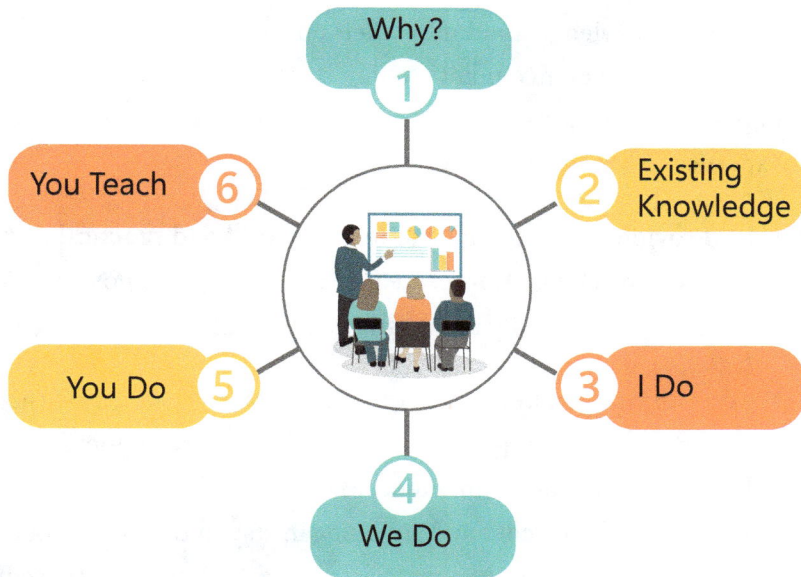

FIGURE 2.4: Adult learning loop of the adaptive leader.
((Adapted from (Gallagher, 1983) (Frey, 2013))

The process is simple, it is an excellent system for adaptive leaders to practice and form new capabilities in wearing the train and support hats. Let's work through the steps:

1. **Why:** When entering training with an individual or team, first ask them why they believe learning this process or topic is important. This provides the learner with instant autonomy, where they can otherwise feel anxious about losing control and being at the mercy of a teacher. Asking them *why* initially builds engagement and motivation.

2. **Existing knowledge:** Before you try to teach an adult anything, ask them what existing knowledge they have on the topic or process. It is disrespectful to assume adults know nothing about a subject or process you are about to teach them. This step draws out their knowledge and builds their engagement. It provides the teacher with reference points to link back to the student's existing knowledge, shows respect, and helps the students link their current expertise to the new learning.

3. **I do:** Provide the learning both in theoretical and practical form. Teach using teaching resources, e.g., work instruction, PowerPoint, etc., and then practically demonstrate the learning.

4. **We do:** Engage the students in the subject or process, giving them part of the process to perform while you wear the support hat to help them truly build competence. Depending on the complexity of the learning, a teacher and student can stay in the We Do phase for an extended period. As a teacher, you are looking for repeatedly demonstrated competence as you increasingly hand over more of the process to them to perform.

5. **You do:** The student has demonstrated repeated competence; it is time for them to take over. This is where the adaptive leader shifts to the coach hat (or direct hat, in extreme circumstances) to support the team member's continued improvement and growth.

6. **You teach:** There is no better way to achieve mastery in an area of skill than to teach it. You Teach can be incorporated into this process as a teach-back step, where the adaptive leader asks the student to teach back the learning once they have demonstrated competence. It can also be incorporated into a system where students become the teachers of future students, learning the adult learning loop, and building their capability in wearing the teach, support, and coach hats.

The focus of teaching varies as leaders progress through the organisational hierarchy. While all leaders must teach culture and improvement, the technical aspects of training differ across levels. Frontline leaders need to focus on process and technical skills, whereas middle and senior leaders concentrate on leadership, management, strategy, and project management skills.

Leaders of leaders are responsible for teaching, supporting, and coaching culture and improvement across all five hats of adaptive leadership. At any leadership level, the adult learning loop enhances teaching effectiveness when wearing the teach hat.

Using the teach hat effectively requires leaders to consider the person and context, especially when responding to questions or challenges. While coaching is often recommended, it may not be suitable if the employee has limited knowledge in a particular area. In such cases, the leader should use the teach hat, ask if the employee would like training (particularly for longer-term employees), and arrange a time for it.

Let's explore a case example that highlights the roller-coaster journey I experienced with leaders and the teach hat.

Early in my career, I worked for a mid-tier, family-owned organisation that eventually grew into a large company. In the early days, the organisation experienced rapid growth, doubling in size year after year, an impressive trajectory for a packaging company in a mature market.

We had a strong employee engagement and recruitment system, knowing exactly where to find ideal employees based on cultural alignment and personal traits. The onboarding process was systematic, with structured learning plans spanning 30, 60, 90, 180, and 360 days. Both leadership and the team actively owned the teach hat, relying on the adult learning loop. Very little, if any, training was outsourced to third parties or software systems.

Unfortunately, things changed when a new HR manager joined us. Coming from a much larger organisation that relied heavily on automated, technology-based learning, she introduced software-based learning systems, claiming they would save leaders time and enhance learning content. Around the same time, new external leaders were brought in from larger, brand-name companies where leaders were rarely involved in training. This cultural shift led to the teach hat being outsourced to external parties and online systems.

The impact was swift and severe, employee turnover escalated, defects increased, and the company's growth flatlined.

Years later, I found myself in a meeting with several sales leaders from this organisation to discuss sales training. One of the leaders, Rhonda, had worked with us during the organisation's early days, left for a while, and then returned as a sales leader.

The sales leaders were frustrated by their team's lack of sales skills and asked me to develop and run further sales training. I knew the importance of leaders owning the teach hat. Without it, leaders wouldn't support their teams in bridging the knowing-doing gap, turning learning into actionable habits.

I turned to Rhonda and asked how we had trained team members in the organisation's early days. Her face lit up as she reminisced about those times. She mentioned that while the quality of the training materials, PowerPoints and videos, was average, the learning seemed to resonate with the team. She attributed this to her leader at the time, John, who wasn't the best trainer but made sure the learning stuck.

I asked her to reflect on why this was the case. After a pause, Rhonda realised it was because John provided one-on-one support and coaching after training sessions and joint customer sales calls. John owned the training because he delivered it himself. This ownership naturally extended to supporting and coaching his team, helping them develop new skills and habits.

In that moment, Rhonda had an a-ha moment. She acknowledged, 'I get it; I need to own the training, and the subsequent support and coaching required to help my people grow their skills and capability.'

The sales leaders went on to develop and deliver an excellent training program, providing post-training support and coaching to their teams. This effort played a major role in the organisation's recent growth and profit increases, well above market figures.

SUPPORT HAT

When the support hat is poorly worn, it can have significant consequences. Leaders failing to follow through with practice and skill development after training results in wasted time, effort, and cost. Similarly, neglecting to wear the support hat when an employee is in an emotional state can erode their trust, as they may feel misunderstood or unsupported.

A leader's willingness to provide learning opportunities and offer support during emotional or challenging times is crucial for fostering a culture of engagement, learning, and continuous improvement. Recent studies show that 76% of employees who experience empathy from their leader report being engaged (Bommel, 2024).

The ability to wear the support hat varies among leaders. While some are naturally empathetic and inclined to help team members learn or form new habits, even those with a natural inclination must consistently practice adaptive leadership to keep this hat in place.

When people are not supported or shown empathy in emotional moments, they may feel uncared for or disrespected. For example, a leader who responds to vulnerability with a quick solution (know-it-all) or by taking over (ultimate carer) can leave employees feeling that the leader is self-serving.

Another key aspect of the support hat is fostering team bonds and trust. One of the authors, while on a flight, had a conversation with Bri, a fellow passenger passionate about teamwork and culture. Bri shared his experiences in the military and mining industries, highlighting the value of simple team-building activities like races, building tasks, or playing games. These events allow team members to connect in a neutral, fun environment, building trust and understanding.

Leaders often focus solely on work and productivity, but there is power in using the support hat to create opportunities for employees to connect and co-create culture. Chapter 3 will delve further into this through the Core Belief System.

Let's explore examples of adaptive leaders effectively wearing the support hat, assessing the person, considering the context, and providing the right kind of support.

TABLE 2.3: Person and context—support hat.

Person	Context
Any employee.	They have been through training. They are struggling to put the new learning into practice or have not started to apply the learning at all.
Long-term employee who is usually an energetic personality.	They are looking flat today. You know they are having some issues with their partner at home.
Salesperson.	Just been through training. You are watching them in a joint sales call. You have agreed prior to the call to review their use of the new skills after the sales call.
Direct report who is in a middle management role.	They are excited about a target the team has just hit. It was an ambitious target, the team put a lot of improvement effort into achieving the outcome.

Wearing the support hat well requires leaders to be skilled in several areas:

1. Asking quality open questions and letting the other person talk rather than you.
2. Active listening. Listening to the words a person says. Listening to their tone and looking at their body language to notice what they are feeling.
3. Paraphrasing to show empathy. Being able to state back to the person what you understood they said and how they are feeling. Not jumping in with your own story or experiences.
4. Saying nothing in highly emotional times. Demonstrating through your body language that you are there for them and care.
5. Giving recognition at every opportunity with a focus on the behaviour not just the task.

These five skill areas are powerful when wearing the support hat. When a person is emotional, either negative or positive, these skills tell them that you are there for them, you care for and are focused on them, helping them rather than shifting the conversation to your own experiences or solutions, which is common.

As mentioned in this section, the support hat is worn to assist someone navigate the challenges of forming new habits and skills. Wearing the support hat in this context also requires empathy.

I've often heard leaders say, 'I've trained them; they should be doing it correctly now.' This belief is a fallacy. Teaching a new skill is only the beginning of the learning process. Developing a habit from training can take time, depending on the complexity of the skill and the individual's motivation.

Like everyone, I've worn the support hat both well and poorly. I recall a moment with my son, Charlie, who is passionate about cricket. While teaching him batting techniques, I didn't need the inspire hat, Charlie's motivation was already high. However, I failed to wear the support hat effectively. When Charlie didn't practice as I expected, I switched to the direct hat, which frustrated him and heightened his emotions.

Realising my mistake, I paused, reflected, and switched to the support hat. I apologised for my behaviour and suggested we take a break to let emotions settle. Reflecting further, I considered Charlie's pride in his current skills and the recent emotional moment. I asked if he'd like to video his practice sessions so he could review and learn independently, without my constant feedback.

Charlie agreed, and this approach worked well. He now reflects on his progress, learns effectively, and enjoys the process. His game has significantly improved, tripling his average scores, while his passion for cricket remains strong.

COACH HAT

Great coaches achieve great things; this has been seen repeatedly in sports. Consider the Chicago Bulls' rise to fame in the 1990s, as highlighted in the documentary Last Dance. When Phil Jackson became their coach in 1989, he embodied the adaptive leader, wearing every hat effectively. He shifted the team's purpose from relying on Michael Jordan to fostering a culture where every player's strengths were maximised (Hehir, 2020). His adaptive approach with Dennis Rodman exemplified his ability to consider context and tailor his behaviour.

The coach hat, in leadership terms, differs from that of a traditional sports coach. It represents the behaviour of open questions and inquiry to prompt others to think deeply and solve problems independently. This approach is most effective with experienced individuals pursuing meaningful goals or facing obstacles. Leaders wearing the coach hat ask open-ended questions to help others uncover solutions and grow by addressing challenges themselves.

Not all leaders excel at wearing the coach hat. Many default to the direct or teach hats, dominating conversations even with capable employees. This often stems from a 'know-it-all' mentality, where leaders thrive on the dopamine hit of solving problems themselves. While this behaviour might momentarily boost the leader's confidence, it stifles employees' growth, reduces engagement, and fosters dependency.

This cycle can have devastating effects. Employees in such environments either leave or disengage, bringing only minimal effort to work. The organisation loses untapped potential, undermining its culture of learning, improvement, and innovation.

Let's explore examples of adaptive leaders effectively using the coach hat, assessing the person, context surrounding them, and choosing ideal behaviour to help them grow.

TABLE 2.4: Person and context—coach hat.

Person	Context
Long term employee who is proud of their skills and knowledge.	They have come to you struggling with a challenge they are facing. They are not in a highly emotional state (support hat needed first if highly emotional).

Person	Context
Employee that has recently joined your team from another department.	The new employee has been trained recently in a process. They have come to you with a challenge. You have seen them perform the process several times correctly.
Quieter employee who has good skills and competence.	They are quieter. You tend to find it difficult to not speak over them. You know they have the skill. They are bringing to you an idea of improvement that you feel they could own and manage themselves.
New employee who has an extensive background in your industry. They are an expert in the field and proud of their skills.	You have trained them in the current process and now want to draw on their knowledge and expertise to improve it.

To effectively wear the coach hat, an adaptive leader must be willing to stay quiet and let others do the talking. They need to be skilled at asking open questions and show active listening and empathy, aligning their responses with the coachee's input. A simple way to gauge effectiveness in coaching is by reflecting on who is doing most of the talking during a conversation.

When the coach hat is worn well, the coachee takes the lead in the conversation, creating a pull-based

To effectively wear the coach hat, an adaptive leader must be willing to stay quiet and let others do the talking.

environment where they actively seek out their own learning and solutions. This contrasts with the push-based environment created by the teach and direct hats, where the leader drives the interaction.

Figure 2.5 (below), based on work by Expression for Growth, illustrates the variation in leadership input across the different adaptive leader hats. Leaders should reflect on the percentage of pull-based language they use with experienced employees in stable contexts. Considering which hats they wear most frequently and identifying areas for improvement can significantly enhance their coaching effectiveness.

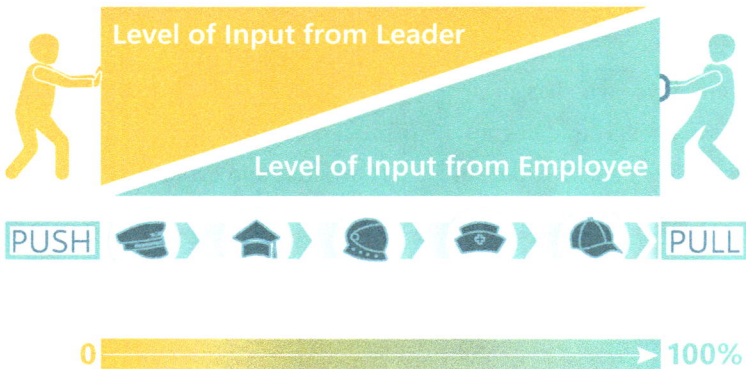

On a scale of 0-100%, where are you currently?

FIGURE 2.5: Push v pull language based on work by expression for growth.

While experts have developed many different coaching models, all of them have the same core ingredients:

1. **Future state:** Use open questions (what, how, why, where, when) to prompt the person to think about the future, the goal they are aiming for, or the outcome they seek from a process. This can be a macro, high-level goal or a smaller one for what they want to occur

in a process or the check in how they felt a specific part of a process is performing.

If the goal or outcome is significant and will take a long time to achieve, it is essential to get the individual to think of a short-term target or outcome they can focus on that will bring them one step closer to the longer-term goal. As humans, we are particularly short-term focused; the more we can take small steps and achieve short-term goals towards larger targets, the more effective we are and the faster we progress.

Ask them questions to understand how inspired and motivated they are in getting to the future target, such as, 'How important it is to you right now to reach that goal or achieve that outcome?'

2. **Current state:** Use open questions to get the individual or team to think about what is occurring now. If there is a problem, use open questions to get them to think of the root causes, such as 'Why it is occurring?' 'What is causing it?'

3. **Explore options:** Use open questions to get the individual to explore as many options as possible to overcome the problem and take a step toward their short-term goal. This is a form of design thinking, asking the individual, 'What else could you do? And what else?' The more ideas you get on the table, the better. The last idea after one final 'what else' could be the gem that unlocks progress.

4. **Action to take:** Once you have all the options on the table, again, use open questions to help the person narrow down the best choice. Techniques such as getting them to explore the value or the level of progress that each idea would provide them toward achieving their goal, together with the complexity and difficulty in implementing each option, can often help people make a desirable choice.

Once you have the designated option, again, use open questions to help them determine a defined action; for example, 'What are you going to do by when?' 'What support, if any, do you require?' 'How and when would you like to check in on progress?'

The most popular coaching model that follows this flow is the GROW model (Whitmore, 1992). GROW stands for Goals, Reality Now, Options, and Way Forward. There are many similar models, as adaptive leaders, we can learn from all these models, create our own approach to practice, improve, and grow.

One of the best transformations I experienced involved a production leader named Trevor, who worked for one of my clients. Trevor was a typical production manager, highly experienced in factory operations but overwhelmed by the whirlwind of daily problems, strategic projects, and new initiatives like equipment installations and product launches.

Trevor's struggle to manage his workload meant he often didn't follow up with his team on issues they raised, leading to disengagement and low psychological safety. Trevor himself was feeling disengaged, overworked, and constantly under pressure.

I don't know what triggered the change in Trevor, but I noticed his behaviour begin to shift. He moved away from a command-and-control, know-it-all leadership style to focusing on coaching and serving his team's growth rather than his own emotions.

Trevor started by wearing the inspire hat. He engaged with his team to understand their goals, purpose, and motivators. Together, they developed an aligned team motto and purpose that connected the team's purpose and goals to the organisations purpose and goals.

He then put on the teach and support hats to help his team learn how to set up visual scoreboards, action trackers, and rapid stand-up meetings to monitor daily progress. Trevor also implemented a system with his leadership team to capture and address frontline issues and ideas transparently.

Embedding these changes wasn't easy. His team's trust and psychological safety had eroded over the years due to unresolved issues and leaders dominating conversations. Trevor continually wore the support and coach hats to rebuild trust, bridge knowledge gaps, and create space for his team to find their voices.

With this foundation in place, Trevor could focus on wearing the coach hat. When team members faced challenges, he asked open-ended questions like: 'What is the goal or outcome you want to achieve?' 'Where are you now, and what's causing this?' 'What options do you have to overcome it?' 'Which option has the highest value and is easiest to implement now?' 'When will we connect back to see what you implemented?'

Trevor became an exceptional coach while also using the other hats to create an environment where his team owned their goals, challenges, and improvements.

During a site tour I hosted for other manufacturers, I witnessed the transformation firsthand. John, one of Trevor's frontline team members, led a meeting, sharing the team's purpose, updating the visual scoreboard, and discussing challenges and solutions, all with confidence and pride. Trevor stayed quiet, letting his team shine.

The visiting companies were amazed by the team's engagement, knowledge, and capability. Their feedback highlighted Trevor's behaviour, keeping quiet and empowering his team.

I know this transformation wasn't quick. Trevor had to let go of his know-it-all and ultimate carer tendencies, embracing a quieter, coaching-focused management style. Seeing the pride on John's face when he received applause from the visitors, and Trevor's subtle smile at his team's recognition was priceless.

I'm proud of what Trevor and his team achieved. Unfortunately, such transformations aren't common in Australia, but I'm passionate about helping more organisations and teams reach this level of success.

We'll dive deeper into coaching in Chapter 9. For now, let's explore wearing the direct hat.

DIRECT HAT

The direct hat plays a vital role in an adaptive leader's toolkit. It ensures safety and addresses poor cultural behaviours promptly before they escalate.

However, leaders often misuse this hat. Some avoid tough conversations because they find them unpleasant and emotionally unrewarding, failing to form the habit of wearing the direct hat. Others overuse it, dominating meetings, suffocating their team, and leaning into ultimate carer or know-it-all tendencies for the emotional satisfaction of helping or sharing their knowledge.

Overusing the direct hat damages psychological safety and trust within teams. Team members may feel undervalued, believing their ideas and skills are unappreciated. This can lead to disengagement or attrition, further reinforcing poor leadership behaviours.

Despite these challenges, the direct hat has critical moments where its use is essential. Let's explore scenarios where leaders thoughtfully assess the person and context, then choose to wear the direct hat.

TABLE 2.5: Person and context—direct hat.

Person	Context
Anyone.	They are at risk of hurting themselves, others, machinery, or the environment.
Anyone.	You have just seen or heard that the individual is doing something that goes directly against your team's purpose, values, and principles (core belief system/team charter).
Longer term skilled employee.	The employee is highly experienced. They have done the process a thousand times before. You have worn the support and coach hats multiple times in recent history on this same topic.
Anyone.	The team member has committed to a clear action and timeline. They have moved the delivery date two or three times for that action/commitment with no explanation.

The greatest adaptive leaders understand when to bring a harder edge to their approach. The direct hat is straightforward to wear in safety or environmental impact contexts, leaders should act quickly to remove people or hazards from harm's way and move toward containment steps without delay.

In cultural moments, wearing the direct hat requires leaders to work with their team to establish a team charter, a shared cultural system with clear ideal behaviours of focus that empowers everyone to use the direct hat respectfully to uphold culture. The ideal behaviours defined in a team charter enables this as behaviours are specific, there is less grey zone that can occur when a team is purely referencing values to lead culture.

The next chapter delves into individual, team, and organisational core belief systems. For individuals, this refers to their core purpose and values. Once a team develops its core belief system, often represented as a team charter, any team member can confidently wear the direct hat when cultural alignment is at stake.

As with the coach hat, there are many structured approaches for wearing the direct hat and providing feedback. Typically, these all follow a similar sequence:

1. **Ask Permission:** Unless there is a safety risk, ask permission to chat. Asking permission diffuses emotion and shows respect even though you are dealing with a cultural problem. You don't want the other person getting too emotional at any stage in the conversation, as this stops them from thinking and learning from the interaction.

2. **Context:** What is the context of what you observed? Where was it? When did it occur? How often did you see or hear about it? Who was involved?

3. **Behaviour:** What are the specific behaviours you saw the person do? Describe it as you saw it.

4. **Impact/risk:** What was the effect or could have been the impact of the behaviour?

5. **Listen:** Listen to the other's view of what happened. Align with them based on their feedback.

6. **Actions:** What actions will be taken to avoid this occurring again? Be sure to capture these precisely and define a time to connect for an update.

Also, similarly to the coach hat, there are many feedback models an adaptive leader can research and learn from to create their own process to practice and improve over time.

With any conversation using the direct hat, there are two sides to the equation: how we deliver the feedback (which the six points above help to do effectively) and how we receive feedback.

Improving how we receive feedback has been researched heavily. The old saying that feedback is a gift is prevalent. A simple way to help yourself and your team improve how you receive feedback is to think of this acronym GIFT:

Gain an awareness of your emotional triggers. In the next chapter, we will explore your core belief system, which is at the heart of your emotional triggers, both positive and negative.

Inquire to understand the feedback you are receiving more deeply. Asking the person giving the feedback to explain more about the feedback broadens our knowledge of the feedback. We learn from it more deeply.

Find alignment. Give feedback, giving your views and side of the story. Listen to their subsequent responses and find alignment.

Thank them for the feedback and act. This is truly the approach of seeing feedback as a GIFT and using what has been learned from it to improve. Again, actions need to be specific and potentially include a feedback loop to reconnect and check up on progress.

When adaptive leaders improve how they give and receive feedback, they amplify the level of constant learning and psychological safety within a team. This is a powerful component of an adaptive leader wearing the direct hat well. We will explore GIFT, giving and receiving feedback, more in Chapter 9.

In the Inspire hat section, we introduced the case example of Anthony. The relationship formed between our author, Anthony, and the other people in the team led to a psychologically safe environment where constructive feedback was seen as a GIFT. Our author and Anthony would regularly seek feedback from each other by asking specific questions, such as 'Yesterday in that meeting, how did I go keeping quiet and letting others talk?'

In these environments, especially when team members actively seek feedback, the direct hat can be worn more often. You can't rapidly take a team straight from a low level of psychological safety, with no one exchanging feedback, to this level. You know your team is entering the high-performance zone when you get to this level.

These are the five hats our authors have found that the most successful adaptive leaders wear, achieving the greatest ideal results in their teams and organisations.

Throughout the remainder of this book, we will explore the different contexts where an adaptive leader can switch between these hats to serve the other person and help them grow towards their full potential. We have mentioned the core belief system within this chapter, which we will explore more deeply in chapter 3, as it plays an influential part in an adaptive leader's ability to pause, think, and respond, and plays a significant part in building and leading culture and performance.

CASE STUDY: MAURO NEVES CEO INCITEC PIVOT

Mauro Neves grew up and entered the workforce in Brazil, starting in the mining and resource industry. Early on in his career, he became passionate about continuous improvement but faced resistance to adopting continuous improvement techniques within mining. The continuous improvement techniques he was trying to implement were prominent within the automotive industry, manufacturing but not mining.

Several years into his career Mauro had the opportunity to visit Toyota's Motomachi production plant in Japan. During the site visit, Mauro saw all the great tools and techniques of continuous improvement, all the things Toyota were famous for implementing. He was desperate to get a few minutes with a senior leader of the Toyota Production System for the site to get hold of their TPS manuals and details on how it is deployed. The moment came when he found himself with the exact leader he wanted to talk to. He asked the TPS leader if he could get the TPS manual and plan details on how it is deployed and implemented. The leader looked at him and said he knew a person in Brazil who led the Ford production system, he could provide him with manuals of their program. Mauro was stunned; he had travelled to Japan, spent all this money, and invested all this time to be told to return to Brazil and talk to Ford. The Toyota leader must have seen the confusion on Mauro's face. He said to him, Mauro, if you want manuals, it is best to get manuals from a manufacturer in Brazil; they are in your language and will provide you with what you are looking for. Continuous improvement is not about manuals and plans. It is about culture, a way of working rather than systems, processes, and tools. It clicked for Mauro; as a leader, he had been so focused on tools and techniques, implementing the latest process or tool rather than culture. This was a turning point for Mauro's leadership career.

Around this time, Mauro landed a job as an asset president at one of our world's largest mines. The site had some challenges, particularly in safety and industrial relations. Mauro was challenged; he wanted to improve things for the people he was serving. Mauro embraced being an adaptive leader who serves the growth of others.

Mauro and his leadership team focused on creating an on-site bottom-up continuous improvement approach that engaged every employee's heart, body and mind. Mauro conducted many look, listen, learn visits to the front line, went to lunchrooms at break time, went to front-line work areas and engaged with employees to understand the challenges they were facing and their ideas on how they could improve culturally. As previously mentioned, a high level of industrial action was occurring when Mauro joined the organisation. He admits there was some initial tension around what he would be caught up in and what would be targeted at him when he went to the front line. This came to the fore when he met a group of front-line employees who said directly to him that they wanted to meet with him. Mauro thought to himself, what do I have to lose? When he met with the small group, he found that they didn't want to beat him up about pay rates and other gripes; they wanted to talk to him about some improvements they felt would help with safety and the flow of work around the site. Mauro lived being an adaptive leader in that moment; Mauro paused, thought about the people he was with and the context surrounding them. They were longer-term employees who seemed engaged and wanted to make a difference; he considered the context that they could be the starting point for their cultural and performance improvement. Mauro chose the coaching hat and said to them, 'What if I give you the time, authority and resources to go and fix those problems?'. Now they were silent; no one had ever said that to them before; one of them smiled and said why not? Let's give it a go!

This small group of employees became the site's pioneers. They kicked off the small autonomous team approach on-site to embrace continuous improvement and make a difference for themselves and others. Mauro kicked up his adaptive leader approach, wearing the inspire, support and coach hats with this team to ensure they felt supported, issues were overcome, and their efforts were promoted across the site and with his leadership team. Mauro focused on training his leadership team on the approach through leading by example and running presentations led by the pioneer group and others as they made improvements on-site. The work of the pioneer group became well-known, and other small teams started to form. It was an opt-in approach; employees were not forced to form autonomous small improvement teams. Each team formed was given strong adaptive leader support from Mauro and the leadership team. All hats of the adaptive leader were worn (limited direct hat) to build team inspiration, capability and help them overcome challenges. Mauro's leadership team started to measure the number of autonomous improvement teams active on-site. They actively avoided measuring dollars saved or productivity gained through the improvement efforts, although they knew this was large. They wanted to focus on the leading measures, the true measures that indicated the movement was gaining momentum.

Mauro mentions that this was not a quick fix; it was five years of effort, starting from the pioneer team and ending with the site winning the prestigious Shingo Prize for Enterprise Excellence. Mauro is now the CEO of Incitec Pivot, a global leader in the resources and agriculture sectors. Mauro will continue to lead transformations as he did in the mining sector to help engage people at work, bring out their creativity and energy through being an adaptive leader. This is an extract of the full case study that can be found at www.leadingexcellencebook.com.

KEY TAKEAWAYS TO PUT INTO PRACTICE THAT WILL DRIVE A HIGH PERFORMING, ENGAGED CULTURE

1. The greatest leaders in the world in any organisation are constant learners and adaptive.
2. The adaptive leader's five hats of primary learning and skill development are inspire, teach, support, coach, and direct.
3. The direct hat can be easily overused by the ultimate carer or a know-it-all leader; however, it is an essential hat, especially when considering safety and poor cultural behaviour.

ACTIVITY 2

Conduct this initial survey to explore your strengths and opportunities around the five adaptive leader hats. Consider which hats are most vital for you to improve your capabilities now. We will explore this area further at the end of the book.

Place a tick in the box that most closely matches your view of yourself. If you feel comfortable doing so, it's always a good idea to sense check your self-assessment with a trusted colleague.

TABLE 2.6: Adaptive leader 5 hat maturity review.

ADAPTIVE LEADER HAT	MATURITY				
	1	2	3	4	5
Direct					
Support					
Teach					
Inspire					
Coach					

1. Need to get this hat
2. Started to practice
3. Use regularly
4. Recognised as proficient
5. Lead by example and coach others

3

CORE BELIEF SYSTEM

The highest performing organisations in the world have been able to create and sustain an engaged, continuously improving, and innovating culture at all levels of the organisation.

These organisations understand that:

1. Ideal results require ideal behaviours.
2. Purpose and systems drive behaviours.
3. Principles inform ideal behaviours.

These are the three insights of organisational excellence that the Shingo Institute, based out of John M. Huntsman School of Business, discovered when they were comparing organisations that have sustained cultures of excellence with those that have peaked and then declined.

While the three insights may appear simple, they are not easy to achieve.

Insight 1: Ideal results require ideal behaviours. Organisations achieve ideal results through their employees exhibiting ideal behaviours. This is logical: if employees are engaged, competent, constantly learning and improving, and demonstrating ideal behaviours, an organisation will have a great culture and achieve remarkable results.

Insight 2: Purpose and systems drive behaviours. Aligned purpose within an organisation fuels the energy and drive for employees to continually enhance their skills and adapt their habits, fostering a culture of continuous improvement and innovation. When a meaningful purpose is ingrained throughout the organisation, it not only provides the 'why' behind the change but also ignites the necessary emotional and energetic commitment to sustain progress over time. Systems refers to the interconnected processes, policies, machines, and software that make up an organisation. These systems will drive behaviours. A simple example is the measurement, reward, and recognition system/process. How we measure, reward, and recognise people in an organisation will drive behaviours for the better or worse. We will explore this in more detail in chapter 10.

Insight 3: Principles inform ideal behaviours. This insight refers to the culture we have defined, put on the wall, and then have either forgotten about or actively live daily. The *Oxford Reference* defines organisational culture as the 'values, customs, rituals, attitudes, and norms shared by members of an organisation' (Oxford University Press, 2024). The key word in this description is 'shared'. Principles are those cultural rules we live by that inform our behaviour. In chapter 1 we explored the case study of Rob Telford and Yandi. The Yandi site defined their principles together:

1. It's the human moments that count.
2. We are all mates, have each other's back, and keep each other safe.
3. The standard you walk past is the standard you accept.

The principles implemented at Yandi (BHP case study chapter 1) served as a foundation for fostering ideal behaviours, resulting in a significant cultural and performance shift. The key to principles lies in their embodiment through daily actions.

When leaders genuinely believe in principles, their behaviours move beyond compliance and become part of their identity, making their leadership authentic and compelling. Later in this chapter, individual core beliefs and the behaviours they inspire will be explored in greater depth.

Many organisations struggle with conflicting team cultures, where misaligned values and attitudes create dysfunction. Edgar Schein, a renowned expert in organisational culture, aptly observed: 'The only thing of real importance that leaders do is to create and manage culture. If you do not manage culture, it manages you, and you may not even be aware of the extent to which this is happening.'

As referenced in Chapter One, Gallup reports that only 23% of employees are engaged at work (2023), often due to negative, misaligned cultures. An organisation can be likened to a coral ecosystem, many organisms working in harmony to thrive. Similarly, organisations excel when individual core beliefs align, fostering engagement and driving exceptional performance.

CORE PURPOSE AND VALUES

Understanding how an individual's culture is formed and governed provides insight into the source of an organisation's culture. For leaders, recognising their own emotional triggers enables them to stay in conscious thought, pausing, thinking, and choosing the right hat for any given person or context.

To visualise how an organisation's culture is shaped by individuals' core purpose and values, the authors collaborated with neuroscientist Professor Dr. Mark Williams and organisational psychologist Lawry Scandar. Dr. Williams, author of The Connected Species (2023), focuses on human connection and its evolution, while Scandar specialises in improving individual and collective cultures within organisations.

Together, they explored what drives emotions and behaviours, both positively and negatively, and what lies at the heart of human identity. This collaboration resulted in the core belief system model illustrated in Figure 3.1.

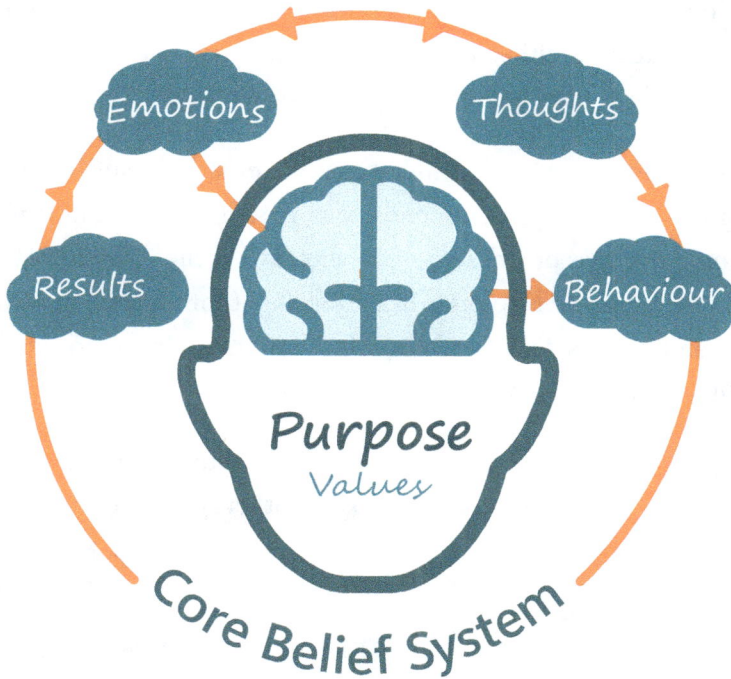

FIGURE 3.1: Core belief system.

At the centre of the core belief system are two key elements: core purpose and core values. Core purpose serves as a north star, a directional, emotion-based driver influencing emotions, thoughts, and behaviours. Core values act as foundational pillars defining who an individual is.

Surrounding this core is the dynamic relationship between emotions and thoughts, which drive each other in a cyclical chain reaction. A triggered emotional response, whether from an event, memory, or thought can lead to a cascade of emotions and subsequent behaviours. For instance, thinking about a favourite food may trigger positive emotions, leading to the behaviour of seeking and consuming it.

Behaviours, in turn, drive results, which can loop back to impact emotions, creating either positive or negative cycles. As outlined in Shingo Insight 1, ideal behaviours lead to ideal results.

However, there is a direct link between emotions and behaviour through the brain, bypassing conscious thought. Overstimulation of emotions, positive or negative, can shut down the conscious brain, leading to automatic responses like fight, flight, or freeze. For leaders, understanding this tendency is critical for managing emotions and choosing the right behavioural 'hat' to serve others effectively.

Pausing to think before acting enables leaders to adapt and respond consciously, improving their ability to help others grow (see Figure 3.2).

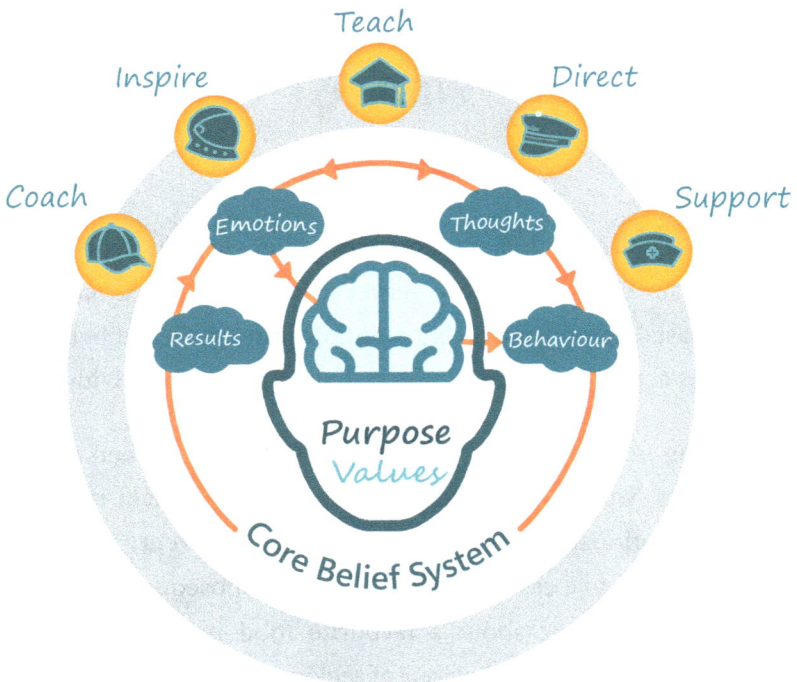

FIGURE 3.2: Core belief system and 5 behavioural hats of the adaptive leader.

Controlling emotions enables leaders to think clearly and adapt to serve others' growth effectively. The challenge arises when self-awareness is lacking, often due to autopilot behaviours or emotional interference. Dr. Mark Williams, in the book's foreword, likens the conscious brain to a rider and the subconscious brain to an elephant. When the rider is in control, they can guide behaviours to achieve ideal results. If the rider loses control, the elephant's emotional impulses can lead to actions that negatively impact others and produce poor outcomes.

Consider a time at work when anxiety or stress made your thoughts foggy and confused. Compare this to moments of calm and focus, where clarity and creativity flow. The first step in managing emotions is understanding personal emotional drivers. By discovering core purpose and values, individuals can identify what triggers emotions, both positively and negatively, and learn to maintain a calmer, more thoughtful state.

Understanding core purpose and values is a straightforward process. The following sections guide readers through this discovery.

Discovering your core purpose

Everyone has a core purpose in life, though it may change over time. The key question is whether one is aware of their core purpose. Gaining this awareness provides numerous benefits:

1. Understanding emotional triggers.
2. A focus point for motivation and inspiration.
3. Guidance through tough times.
4. Clarity to prioritise what truly matters.
5. Improved ability to identify alignment or misalignment with others and organisations.

These benefits underscore the value of uncovering one's core purpose. A straightforward process can help anyone explore this deeper understanding (see Figure 3.3).

Who and what do I serve ?	What do they value ?	What are my goals ?	Why are these my goals ?
Family Leaders People Planet	Love, Fun, Growth, Success, Safety, Health, Morale, Life	Successful Father, Author & Consultant	See Fig 3.4 for Example

FIGURE 3.3: Core purpose discovery steps.

To explore one's core purpose, it's best to follow these steps in sequence:

1. **Who and what do you serve?** Identify those you serve, such as family, employees, customers, or the community, and what you serve, including the planet or assets important to you.

2. **What do they value?** Reflect on what these individuals or entities value and what they consider important from you.

3. **What are your goals in life?** Determine the measurable outcomes you want to achieve based on who and what you serve and they value.

4. **Why are these your goals?** Link your goals with those you serve and explore why they matter to you. Keep questioning each response to uncover your deeper purpose.

Figure 3.4 provides a practical example from one of the authors.

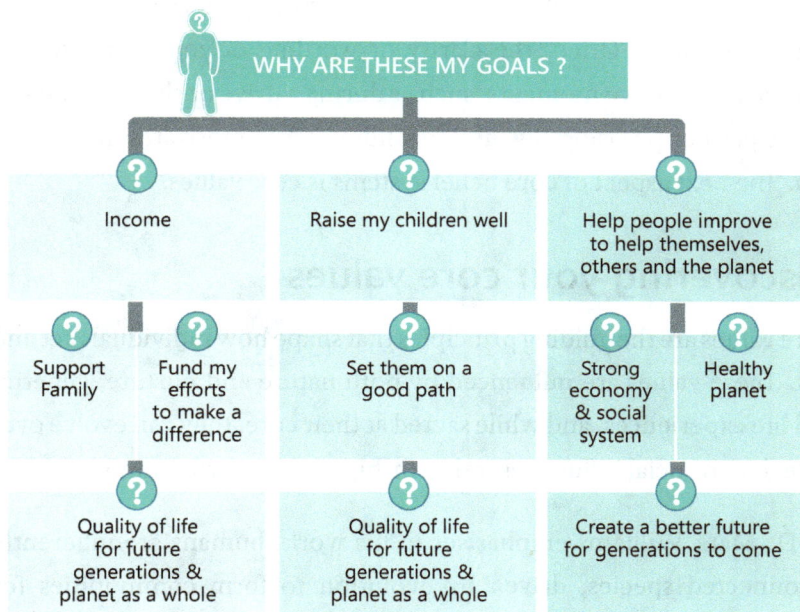

FIGURE 3.4: Core purpose discovery example.

Working through these steps clarifies what is truly important in life. People are naturally inclined to serve, whether it's themselves or others, driven by a mix of intrinsic and extrinsic motivations. There is no right or wrong in this; it simply reflects individual preferences.

By considering the values of those we serve, we can align with them and deliver meaningful value. Reflecting on goals from this perspective fosters a holistic view, avoiding the tunnel vision that prioritises one area over others.

Asking 'why' multiple times about what you serve, and your goals helps uncover the deeper emotional drivers of your core purpose. For example, one author identified their purpose as *creating a better future for generations to come.*

This process is not about finding an instant core purpose but beginning to understand it. Often, the clarity or wording of your purpose will emerge in reflective moments, such as during a drive or shower. The key is not perfect phrasing but understanding what motivates and drives you. The next aspect of core belief systems is core values.

Discovering your core values

Core values are the guiding principles that shape how individuals act and feel. These values are influenced by both nature and nurture, genetics and life experiences, and while sacred at their core, they can evolve over time due to social influences, relationships, and external stimuli.

As Dr Mark Williams emphasises in his work, humans are inherently a connected species, driven by evolution to form communities for survival. However, this drive can sometimes lead individuals to adapt their core values to align with the broader group's, even in extreme historical examples of collective behaviour.

Often, core values are not immediately visible, yet they deeply influence decisions and actions. For instance, someone with honesty as a core value may experience strong emotional reactions to dishonesty.

Understanding core values offers several benefits:

1. Greater insight into emotional triggers, enabling better emotional regulation and adaptive behaviour.
2. Deeper understanding of motivations, thoughts, and behaviours.
3. A clear framework for navigating decisions and future actions.
4. Awareness of social influence on values, allowing for intentional sustenance or adaptation of core principles.

The first step to uncovering core values is to reflect on emotions using the core value discovery process (see Figure 3.5).

FIGURE 3.5: Core value discover process.

To explore core values, consider the following steps:

1. **Identify Emotional Triggers**

    Reflect on instances where you were emotionally triggered by someone, either positively or negatively. These moments often relate to alignment or conflict with your core values. List these triggers, prioritising them based on their emotional impact.

2. **Examine the Cause**

    For each emotional trigger, ask yourself why it impacted you. Continue questioning the 'why' behind each response until you notice recurring themes or memories. Often, pivotal moments from your past significantly shape your values. For instance, I recalled a memory of my grandfather teaching the importance of respect, which became a foundational value for me.

3. **Hypothetical Scenario Value Discovery**

Imagine being confined with others for an extended period. What behaviours or values would you expect them to demonstrate? These preferences reveal the values you hold most dear.

By working through these steps, you can uncover the core values driving your emotions and behaviours. This process may take time, but the goal is to gain a deeper understanding of your values rather than defining them perfectly. These values serve as a guide for interpreting your feelings and actions towards others.

CASE STUDY: SIGNET PTY LTD GRADUATE PROGRAM

Signet Pty Ltd stands out as an organization that prioritizes helping employees discover their core belief system early on in their careers, particularly through its graduate program. For many individuals at Signet, their journey with the company begins through this program, joining the organisation often just before or after their university graduation.

Lasting two years, Signet's graduate program is more than just an entry point; it's a comprehensive immersion into the company's culture. The program includes various off-site events geared towards fostering connections among graduates, leaders, and learning collaboratively. One standout event is dedicated to exploring culture, kicking off with a deep dive into the discovery of each graduate's core belief system. Here, they collectively grasp the significance of core purpose and values, following the steps outlined in this chapter to uncover their own core belief system.

Signet's commitment to this approach stems from recognizing the profound impact of purpose and values on overall organizational performance. The focus on cultural alignment is paramount, guiding graduates to understand their core belief systems and how they align with their teammates and the organisation.

During these sessions, graduates openly explore and share their core purpose and values, exploring alignment with one another and the organisation's overarching mission. For individuals like Tom Connolly (A recent Signet Graduate), this process proved pivotal in shaping his engagement, motivation, and subsequent performance at work. Tom's realisation that his core purpose revolves around aiding others in their growth and achieving together. He found that his purpose aligned with his team members and Signet's organisational purpose of Helping Australia Compete.

Moreover, Tom discovered a strong alignment between his core values and the organisations which are Honor, Ownership, Commitment, Change for Strength and Diligence. This helped Tom form a cultural bond with his team and organisation. It provided him a level of comfort in joining the right organisation, and fostered motivation through understanding his purpose and how he could bring this to life and live it at Signet.

We will now explore your core belief system and others, similar to the approach taken by Signet early on as part of their graduate program.

Your core belief system and others

Every individual has a core belief system, whether they are conscious of it or not. When two people's core beliefs align, they often find connection, trust, and mutual goals. Conversely, misaligned beliefs can create division and misunderstanding. For instance, individuals focused on environmental sustainability may align, while someone focused solely on personal wealth and power may not share their path.

It's not about who is right or wrong; perspectives differ based on personal lenses. Core beliefs drive emotions, motivations, and behaviours. Misalignment can confuse or frustrate, but instead of reacting emotionally, it's critical to understand the differences and respond thoughtfully.

Leaders can foster alignment by seeking to understand others' core beliefs, showing empathy, and sharing their own values with vulnerability. This approach builds trust and rapport, opening the door to mutual understanding and potential change. Emotional reactions rarely resolve misalignment, but awareness and thoughtful behaviour can influence and bridge gaps.

Many successful leaders and organisations define values and ideal behaviours to shape and improve their culture. Aligning core beliefs is a key step toward fostering collaboration, trust, and performance.

CASE STUDY: WOODS WAY

One of our authors got a call one day from the people and culture leader, Gary Bartlam, of Woods Group, a regional Australian company with its head office in Goondiwindi, five hours inland from the nearest city, Brisbane. Gary was looking for a provider of continuous improvement training for their people. He initially thought, 'Oh no, not another company looking to train their people in continuous improvement skills without focusing on strategy, culture, and leadership to ensure it sustains.'

On arriving at Goondiwindi, our author sat down and listened to CEO Tom Woods introduce the event. With passion in his voice, Tom stood up and said, 'We need to bring wealth and prosperity to regional Australia, the towns we love, and the towns we raise our families in. Too much of our produce is shipped into the cities and overseas without being value-added. We are dominated by market pricing and receive the lowest margins for all our hard work. Woods will grow regional Australia by feeding the world with value-added manufactured products, products we have processed, packaged, and added value. This will help us grow our community of Gundi for our families and future generations.

The room was silent; our author was stunned. Tom had presented his purpose and vision with such enthusiasm and clarity, and in a way that was so relevant to his people, that we were all speechless. Finally, the applause started. Everyone was fired up. The excitement in the room was terrific and it felt like Woods Group had just won the local football final.

Our author ran the training and then started to coach and support Tom, Gary, and the rest of the leadership team on the opportunity they had to define the Woods Way and lead excellence as they expanded throughout regional Australia. The Strategic and Cultural Woods Way (Core Belief System) was developed in collaboration with all employees. Small focus groups with front line leadership and employees were held to define their values and ideal behaviours. A representative from each focus group then gathered with senior leadership to define the Woods Way:

Purpose

Grow Regional Australia by Feeding the World

Values and Ideal Behaviours

Do it right the first time:

- Be hard on the process not the person & get to the root cause.
- We have a process & follow it to ensure quality and safety.
- We call it as it is, set a standard, and be honest with ourselves and each other.

Grow our capability:

- Develop career pathways, train and coach to The Woods Way.
- Lead from the front to learn and help our team grow.
- Tell me and I forget. Teach me and I remember. Involve me and I learn.

Be part of the team:

- Work as a team towards our goals and scoreboard to win.
- Play to our strengths and support each other's weaknesses.
- Recognise and celebrate each other's achievements

Continuously improve and innovate:

- Be proactive not reactive, plan and prioritise for today and the future.

- Communicate regularly and work with everyone in the supply chain to create rhythm.
- Be courageous, chase your dreams and goals.

Respect everyone:

- Value and empower our people to achieve great things.
- Don't ask someone to do what you wouldn't do yourself
- Understand and respect our internal and external customers.

Woods's leaders are now delivering training on the Woods Way, building mastery in their skills, and supporting the development of adaptive leaders who serve the growth of others.

Woods now has the centrepiece of their organisational ecosystem that can guide and support everything they do to grow their people through improving their ability to lead the Woods Way as adaptive leaders.

CASE STUDY: SUPER COACH WAYNE BENNETT

With 12 Grand Final appearances, eight premiership wins across three clubs, and a history of international success, Wayne Bennett's coaching legacy is remarkable. His achievements often came with underdog teams in the fiercely competitive sport of Rugby League, a testament to his unique leadership approach.

Four core behaviours underpin his success: understanding individuals, defining purpose and culture, leading by example, and continuous improvement.

Understand and adapt to the individual

Wayne prioritises understanding players on a personal level, fostering trust and respect. Whether it's sharing meals, sitting next to a player on the bus, or relating to their background, he builds relationships based on humility and care. His philosophy, 'They don't care until they know you care,' encapsulates this approach. By connecting with players, he discovers what inspires them and uses this knowledge to help them grow.

Define and align purpose and culture

Purpose and culture are central to Wayne's teams. In 1989, the Broncos' Creed was created, setting behavioural expectations such as personal responsibility and preparedness. This clarity extends to holding players accountable. A well-known incident involved fining two players, not for partying excessively but for failing to intervene with teammates. His belief that 'the standard you walk past is the standard you accept' reinforces his commitment to cultural accountability.

Lead by example.

A common statement Wayne makes is 'a true leader does not see themselves as a leader. They become one by the quality of their actions and the honesty of their intent.'

Wayne believes in not asking anyone to do anything he wouldn't do himself. He leads with respect, staying around after practice to help the trainers and groundsman pick up all the gear. Even though Wayne is now 74, he still joins in gruelling preseason training sessions. Wayne exudes leading from the front with respect. This behaviour builds the ultimate respect in his team members towards him.

Constantly look, listen, learn, and improve

Wayne was not born a great coach; he has not had a smooth ride. His coaching career has been a constant experiment with constant learning. He understands the player individually and his team as a whole; he is constantly alert and learning about them. He then improves himself, his approach to ensure success.

One example is Wayne's time coaching St George Illawarra (Andrews, 2023). St George had a proud history of winning the premiership for many years running throughout the 50s, 60s and 70s. The challenge was that the club had not won a title for many years. Wayne noticed early on that the player's energy and behaviour slumped if winning the premiership was mentioned. He knew that the pressure of past success and recent failures weighed heavily on the team. Wayne implemented a new ideal behaviour for their season: no one would mention the finals or winning the premiership at any stage. They would focus on leading behaviours like keeping teams under 16 points through high-quality defence. The story of St George's 2010 campaign culminated at halftime in the grand final, down 8 points to 6 against the Sydney City Roosters. Wayne considered his team, the context surrounding them and walked into the dressing room at halftime, stood silently in front of the players for what would have seemed like an eternity to them and said, 'Why don't you start being St George? Why don't you start being the team that got us here. The team I am watching is not St

George'. He walked out; the players were stunned. Then, one of the players rallied and fired up, which created a chain reaction across the team room. St George won that final 32 – 8, keeping the Roosters scoreless in the second half.

Wayne has helped so many young men, who otherwise may not have reached their potential and whose lives could have worked out so differently. Wayne's career statistics are impressive, yet our author is sure the players and his family he has served make him the proudest.

KEY TAKEAWAYS TO PUT INTO PRACTICE TO DEFINE YOUR CORE BELIEF SYSTEM:

1. We all have a core belief system that drives our emotions. Understanding this can help us effectively control our emotions, stay in a place of thought, and be adaptive leaders.

2. Understanding other people's core belief systems can help us to understand them more deeply. This knowledge helps us to adapt our approach and guide them towards their full potential.

3. It is our behaviours and how we make people feel through these that define us as leaders. Defining ideal behaviours as a team/organisation provides us a guiding light to be adaptive to improve ourselves and others.

ACTIVITY 3

Use table 3.1 to explore ideal behaviours within your team or with a front line team.

TABLE 3.1: Activity 3.

ACTION	IDEAL BEHAVIOUR	LEADERSHIP HAT(S)
Set a meeting with your team or a small team of front-line employees. Get them to imagine we are at a team lunch in 5 years' time talking about the amazing culture we have. Ask them to describe what we would see people doing? Capture the information they provide using Post It Notes that can then be grouped into common themes. Identify a few ideal behaviours the team capture.	Leaders seeking to engage employees and explore ideal behaviours. Leaders showing curiosity and learning from others.	Inspire Support Coach

4

RESPECT, HUMILITY AND TRUST

One of our core beliefs is that hardly anyone comes into work to deliberately do a bad job. Most people want to do a great job, do something they can be proud of, and feel valued for it. If we look at the world of work in this way, then we start to understand that our job as leaders is to help people to do this. This belief stems from some simple but very powerful personal values. These values are at the heart of our core belief system.

RESPECT EVERY INDIVIDUAL

When people give and receive respect, an energising environment is created that enables everyone to fully develop to their own full potential. They feel empowered to improve themselves and the processes that they 'own'. They are motivated to engage with their hearts and minds, not just with their hands, in that effort. Respect should be shown to every individual (including oneself), regardless of their level or position. (adapted from The Shingo Institute Shingo Model Booklet).

Respect can be thought of as the courage to be acutely aware of the wake we leave after interacting with others. Whether we are technically correct or not, our messages simply will not be heard if we are disrespectful in the way we deliver them. People will remember how we made them feel for much longer than they will remember what we said.

> Respect, though, does not mean avoiding tough conversations.

Respect, though, does not mean avoiding tough conversations. Quite the opposite. It is more disrespectful to pretend everything is fine when there is a source of tension. Equally, it is disrespectful to make decisions that affect people while trying to 'protect' them by keeping anything a secret.

It is important to remember that someone with a high level of authority can sometimes be seen as being immune to the consequences of treating people with less respect than we all deserve. Authority comes with responsibility and a need to be even more self-conscious of the impact of one's words and actions. This is because people in authority are less likely to receive meaningful feedback unless they seek it out deliberately.

Respect every individual is about seeing people as people. This may seem simplistic but pause and ask yourself how often you really see and think about the person you are talking to at work as an individual unless they are a close work colleague. Instead, we often think of people by the job they do— 'the data entry clerk' or 'the guy on the shop floor'.

One charity in Australia encourages us to think about 'a person without a home' rather than label someone as homeless. First and foremost, they are a person; and secondly, they don't have anywhere to live. If you pause and think in this way, you will respond emotionally in a very different way to the next person you see without a home.

A fundamental level of respect is that the organisation provides a safe environment with the tools, training, and systems required to enable success. After all, most people come to work wanting to do a good job. Unfortunately, all too often we see people given inadequate training in overly complex processes without the right tools to do the job and then they get blamed when they make a mistake. This is the opposite of respect.

To quote the Shingo Institute:

> When people feel respected, they give not only their hands but also their minds and their hearts. Respect for every individual is manifested when organisations structure themselves to value each individual as a person and nourish their potential.

LEAD WITH HUMILITY

Leading with humility is tough. It requires the strongest of individuals to be prepared to admit that, even though they are a leader, they do not know all the answers and can learn from everyone else around them. It is often misunderstood as servile or soft leadership, but it is not at all. True, leading with humility requires the individual to show vulnerability, but the ability to do this requires courage and strength of character. We will explore the importance of vulnerability in more detail in chapter 8.

A key aspect of leading with humility is what is often referred to as *leaders who serve*. One way to think about this concept is to recognise that the role of the leader is to serve the managers in the organisation to enable them to serve the team members so that they can better serve the customer.

> Humility is the courage to be curious about ideas, opinions and thoughts that are not your own.

Leaders need to practice being 'egoless'. As a leader, we need to help our people to see how clever they are, not keep showing them how clever we are. We keep our minds open to new ideas and suggestions, recognising that good ideas can come from anyone, anywhere, anytime. We actively seek input from others and actively listen with respect. In the words of Albert Einstein, 'A true genius admits that he/she knows nothing.'

Humility is the courage to be curious about ideas, opinions and thoughts that are not your own. Trust cannot exist without humility. A willingness to demonstrate vulnerability is essential to true humility. Humility is important as a critical aspect for anyone in a position of authority, as it is often the only way to ensure that people can share what they want to share and not what they think their leaders want to hear.

Humble people understand that good ideas can come from anyone, at any time. For example, workers on the floor who are closest to the processes possess vast knowledge and are in the best position to think of ideas that will improve those processes. Leaders who hold on to the myth that they alone can generate good ideas will limit the rate of growth in people and will diminish the rate of process improvement in the organisation. When people know that their leaders want to listen to them, they feel respected and motivated.

TRUST

Trust is the courage to rely on others, and to make it safe for others to rely on you. People *trust* us as we give them *respect* and act with *humility*, showing them that we are willing to listen to and learn from them. We are trustworthy (worthy of their trust) when we keep promises that we make.

The primary difference between a group of employees and an effective team is that effective teams have deep mutual trust. To have an effective team, people must have trust in one another, trust in their leaders, and trust that the organisation will stand behind them. This trust cannot exist unless people are also trusted by their peers, their leaders, and the organisation.

> People *trust* us as we give them *respect* and act with *humility*, showing them that we are willing to listen to and learn from them.

Trust is created when people feel safe. If they do not feel safe, they will do whatever they must to be safe by acting in ways to protect themselves. The principle of trust applies equally to our customers. They are placing their trust in us.

Respect, humility and trust are interwoven. None are fully realised without all being in place.

People, regardless of their professional training or position, sometimes make mistakes. If someone is about to make a mistake, others must feel safe enough to call it to their attention. If there is fear in the room, if people do not feel safe enough to speak out, the result is people who know something but don't say anything. We fail to get their contribution to something that might turn out to be critical to the conversation.

Trust enables asking for, and accepting, feedback so we can learn from one another. This can only happen if people can safely say 'I don't know' and request help without fear of ridicule or being demeaned.

Trust must be earned, and it can take a long time to earn it and minutes to lose it. Key elements of trust are consistency and reliability. In other words, we stick to an agreed path until there is a consensus agreement that change is needed, and we do what we say we are going to do. We are reliable because we keep the promises that we make and demonstrate integrity through our words and actions.

Respect, humility and trust are interwoven. None are fully realised without all being in place.

PSYCHOLOGICAL SAFETY

Safety is a basic requirement of respect. We are not even at the starting block if we have not provided a safe working environment for our people. Whilst there has been fantastic progress made in physical health and safety, with many organisations seeking certification to the international health and safety standard ISO45000 or at least following its recommendations, fewer have yet fully recognised the importance of psychological safety.

The more recent addition of ISO45003 identifies what's needed to support this. Recent work in this area shows that we cannot expect to embed a culture of continuous improvement unless we have a psychologically safe environment. Respect, humility, and trust are foundational to this (*Why Care?* Warner, Greenlee, and Butterworth, Routledge, 2024).

RESPECT, HUMILITY AND TRUST CASE EXAMPLES

CASE STUDY: RESPECT, HUMILITY, AND TRUST NOT IN PLACE

Several years ago, a group CEO asked me to visit his three sites. We were working with him and his team, helping to develop a high-level plan to deeply embed a culture of continuous improvement at the group level. We agreed that our author should visit each of the sites to get a feel for the business. Even though all three were of a similar size and in the same type of industry, there was significant variation in results.

The first site visited was seen as the star performer. It quickly became apparent that the leadership team was dedicated to continuous improvement and had already started to implement a local improvement program with good buy-in; it was well into its second year. Their success was one of the reasons for looking for a group-level approach and it was important to learn what had worked and not force them to start again with something totally different.

The second site had an okay performance, with a solid leadership team who knew they could do a lot better and had a good culture. They had not yet started any formal continuous improvement program. They were, however, very keen to start and had been waiting for the launch from the other group rather than start something and then have to change it.

The third site was seen as underperforming, and it quickly became apparent what the problem was. There were two very strong characters in the leadership team who had no respect for each other and focused more time and energy on how to get one over on the other person than on the overall health of the business.

This was apparent from observing the conversation at the end of a leadership team meeting that was just wrapping up as our author was invited into the board room. There was a total lack of trust and respect, not only for each other but for anyone in the workforce.

Our author asked one of these leaders to take me on a tour of the facility and whilst he clearly thought this was beneath him and he had more important things to do, he reluctantly agreed, making it clear he was only doing so because our author had 'been sent' by the group CEO. There was a definite lack of humility.

The facility was well laid out and had clearly marked green walkways where pedestrians were meant to walk. Our author asked if we needed any hi-vis or hearing protection and got a scornful reply about not needing to bother 'with that rubbish'. As we walked along the marked route at quite a pace, we came across a pallet of raw material that had been left blocking the green lane. My host ignored it, walked into the red zone, and continued. Our author decided to stop and just waited until the host noticed.

He turned around and came back and the conversation went something like this:

Host: What's the matter?

Me, pointing at the pallet: Well, I just wondered if this should be here?

Host: Well, probably not, but you can just walk round it.

Me: Well, I could, but then I haven't got any PPE and, also, I don't think that I should.

Host: Oh, come on. I've just done it. You will be fine.

Me: So, if we just ignore it, what message are we sending?

Host, looking at me as if I'd just crawled out from under a stone: Oh, I see. This is a test, is it? Ok, then, I will deal with it. Wait here and I'll find the supervisor and tell him to get this sorted and discipline who ever left it here. Happy now?

Me: Well, not really. I'm not sure that will fix the problem.

Host: Of course, it will. I guarantee it won't be here by the time we finish our little look round and it will only take me a minute to tell the supervisor to get his act together and tear the forklift driver a new one. Just wait here and I'll be right back.

Me: But wouldn't it be useful to know why it's here?

Host: I know why it's here. Some lazy XXXX couldn't be bothered to put it away properly. They'll soon learn not to do that again.

Me: Could we at least ask the supervisor why it's here, just to make sure?

Host: Well, if you insist. He looked round and caught sight of an operator whose name he didn't know and shouted—'Hey, you. Find Fred and tell him I want him here pronto.'

By this point, our author was feeling rather concerned about several things but mainly about what was going to happen to Fred and his workmate. So, he decided to try and help and persuaded the host to let him ask a few questions before he said anything. Clearly very unhappy, he reluctantly agreed just as Fred hurried up to us.

Me: I shook Fred's hand, which he was not expecting, introduced myself, and explained I was visiting to learn about the site. I said that I was just curious about why this pallet was here.

Fred looked at my host, who just glared at him, then back at me. His response was gold.

Fred: Well, we were just discussing that when I got called over. The thing is, it's come in on the wrong pallet and we can't get it to fit in front of the machine where it's supposed to go. Jamie just dropped it here a few minutes ago to come and find me so we could work out what to do. I know it shouldn't be here, but I think he panicked a bit as he's never had it happen before, and he wasn't sure what to do as he's only been here a couple of weeks. We've discussed and agreed on how to handle it if it happens again and I've reinforced why we can't put stuff in the walkway. We have just agreed on a plan with purchasing about how to use this one and how to get the supplier to sort out the issue. Jamie will be here in a minute to move it to where we've agreed.

Me: Thanks, Fred. That sounds like a great approach. Well done on getting that sorted.

My host just glared at us. Struggling for words, he decided on: Right. Now that's sorted, let's carry on with the tour.

No one can give their best in a culture of fear and recrimination, and it was obvious this site leadership team was not going to successfully lead the implementation of a CI program without a lot of work focused on themselves first.

CASE STUDY: STARTING TO DEVELOP RESPECT, HUMILITY AND TRUST
(Inspire Hat Example)

I was invited to visit a facility by the newly appointed CEO (Mark), who he'd worked with previously. It was his first week in the job and as we walked round the site, it felt like I was going back in time to Victorian England. It was very dark, the workforce looked downtrodden, and there was old equipment and material abandoned everywhere. It had once been a flagship of engineering excellence but now had a workforce a fraction of the size it used to be, a shrinking order book, and more space than they knew what to do with. Everyone seemed to be just waiting for bad news.

We passed one crew operating a machine wearing knee-high rubber boots. We paused and Mark said, 'That's not good.' We walked over to the crew and asked them what was happening. The story they told highlighted the scale of the challenge the site faced. A seal had worn that morning, and they needed to get a job finished so they were manually pouring oil in faster than it was leaking out to keep the machine running. It was a regular occurrence, and they'd even managed to rig up an ingenious system that reused some of the spilling oil.

Mark immediately asked them to stop as it was clearly unsafe and then asked the maintenance manager to make it a priority. The production supervisor came over and advised the machine couldn't stop as a customer order had to be shipped.

Mark's response was, 'I will deal with the customer, and no-one works on that until it's safe to do so.'

As we walked around, Mark said, 'If you thought that was bad, you should see the toilets and dining room facilities that we expect people to use. I wouldn't let my dog use them.'

Mark had been given 12 months to get the site to break even or it would be closed. Much to the shock and outrage of the board, one of his first actions was to totally refurbish the toilets and the changing rooms and provide a clean room for people to eat in.

When this was finished, he called an all-workforce meeting and explained the challenge they had. 'We have 12 months to save this site and our jobs, and together I think we can do that. We need to do three things so that we are no longer losing money in 12 months time:

- Keep each other safe.
- Deliver good quality product, to the customer on time at the right cost.
- Generate more cash so we can invest in improvements.

There was understandably a lot of scepticism about this but what was fascinating was watching people's faces as Mark talked about what was required. He was someone who had already made major changes that had positively impacted on health and safety and had shown respect to everyone in his actions and conversations, and he had been there for less than eight weeks. It was clear many wanted to give him the benefit of the doubt and were prepared to give it a try.

Mark's next action was to engage the whole workforce in a major clean up, with the aim of improving health and safety and generating cash. He had the idea that if they could be better organised, he would have options to turn some of the excess space into revenue opportunities.

He did this with a bold plan. He advised the workforce that he would rent out any space that was created, which would immediately help with the goal of not losing money. In addition, they would raise money from selling redundant equipment and scrap. To allow everyone to see the immediate benefits, 25% of all money raised would be allocated to spend on ideas the workforce came up with for improvements.

The transformation in the workforce was incredible to see and went from strength to strength as the respect, humility, and trust that Mark had shown to the employees permeated throughout the business and became the culture of the site. It was not an easy journey and there were many ups and downs. However, after a lot of hard work and dedication from everyone in the business, they succeeded in breaking even after 12 months. Three years later they were one of the most profitable sites in the group.

CASE STUDY: RESPECT, HUMILITY, AND TRUST IN PLACE

(Inspire, Support, Coach Hat Example)

I visited an organisation where the leaders had embraced the concept of leaders who serve. The leaders genuinely believed their role was to support the workforce to be the best they could be and do a wonderful job for the customer.

They decided to publish their organisational chart as an inverted triangle. The leadership team was shown at the bottom of the triangle and the team members at the top, as the team members have a direct impact on the customer experience in many ways every day. An illustrative example is shown in Figure 4.1 below.

Leaders Who Serve

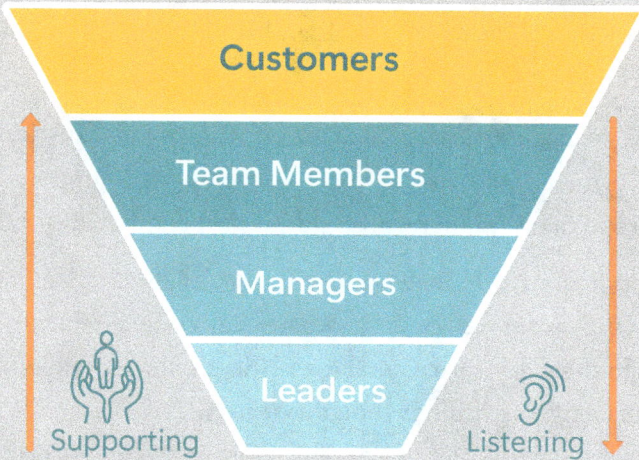

Customers

Team Members

Managers

Leaders

Supporting

Listening

FIGURE 4.1: Leaders who serve—Organisational mindset.

This made a big impression on me but admittedly I was a bit sceptical. They decided to dig deeper and try to understand what this picture really meant. What they came to understand is that the mindset behind the picture was more important than the picture itself.

Their conversations revealed that the workforce genuinely felt that they had a direct impact on the experience of the customer and that their leaders would support any decision they made which resulted in a positive customer and employee experience. It transpired that job titles and expectations around roles had changed. No longer were supervisors overseeing the work that the teams did. Instead, they had become team leaders whose primary role was to coach, develop, and support the team members.

There was a strong focus on continuously developing listening skills throughout the organisation. This is a very powerful and underestimated leadership skill and will be explored in more detail in chapter 9.

Senior managers became leaders of groups of team leaders. Their primary role was to coach, develop, and support team leaders so that they, in turn, could support team members.

Success for a team leader and a group leader was defined as developing teams to the point where they could effectively self-manage their day-to-day activities. This took some time to put in place and was still not thought of as working perfectly even after several years, as the organisation was constantly trying to improve its systems and people development. But it would not have been even possible to contemplate without respect, humility, and trust.

They had developed a very simple mantra about any change that was being discussed by embedding a simple question. At every level, they would ask: will this change make the experience better for our customer and simpler for us? If it doesn't do both, we need to find a different way to do it.

It's not enough just to display the new organisational chart. We've seen that this can generate a huge amount of distrust and cynicism when it is done without the underlying beliefs and behaviours being changed. It should be seen as a picture that demonstrates what has been achieved, not used as something that shows an unrealised aspiration.

Organisations that have developed this culture have leaders who have developed the ability to switch between the different hats and adapt as the context requires. Over time, this ability is embedded as a habit and becomes the natural way things happen. People are promoted who demonstrate respect, humility, and trust and can apply the adaptive leadership hats as needed.

CASE STUDY: RESPECT, HUMILITY, AND TRUST IN PLACE

(Support Hat Example)

One of the most enjoyable things the authors get to do is undertake continuous improvement 'maturity assessments' to help organisations to understand what's working really well in their CI culture and where the opportunities are to take it to the next level. This means we are very lucky to see a lot of great ideas and meet wonderful people from around the world. We all learn something new on every assessment but one conversation from a few years ago has always stuck with us.

We were discussing one organisation's cultural change program with a senior director who had supported her team to achieve some amazing results in transforming a lacklustre division into a high-performing part of the organisation. As we listened to all the wonderful initiatives that had been implemented, we asked her which one she was most proud of. After a short reflection, she said one initiative stood out as a major turning point for the whole program—the one that was a complete failure. She went on to explain that several projects had been very successful, but it wasn't until the first major failure that the team really started to pull together and learn.

They hadn't understood the reasons for their successes and the first failure was a big shock. However, rather than being disheartened, the team decided to review their whole approach. They decided to understand what went wrong using root cause analysis and the voice of the employee and voice of the customer interviews. The leadership team didn't blame anyone but demonstrated genuine humility seeking to understand, reflect, and learn from the experience.

The leader's view was that they learned very little from the initial successes because there had been no need for reflection. The result of the 'failed project' was better teamwork and a greater understanding of how to ensure success. One of the key outcomes was that reflection was built in as a standard step, even when things went well. As a result, any 'failure' was seen as a learning opportunity and approached with humility.

In this example, the leader was mainly wearing the support hat to encourage and motivate her team through an unexpected outcome and then helped coach them through to a different way of thinking.

ACCOUNTABILITY

Having respect, humility, and trust in place does not mean we have a cosy environment with no accountability. In fact, it means quite the opposite. It might seem strange but what we see in organisations where respect, humility, and trust are in place is higher levels of personal accountability. Why is this?

1. Respect, humility, and trust are embedded when organisations develop behavioural expectations that demonstrate these principles. This enables everyone at every level to hold each other accountable for the way they behave.
2. Where these are in place there is a no blame culture. Where there is no blame, people are more open and willing to admit if something hasn't gone as well as they would have liked. The positive, supportive environment means that they accept personal accountability for fixing the issue and/or seeking help on how to fix it.
3. What we also see in these organisations is a greater sense of personal pride where people want to do a great job and help each other do a great job.

BEHAVIOURS

As we discussed in chapter 3, behaviours underpin our personal and organisational core belief systems. One way to start changing our thinking on behaviours is by focusing on a specific belief or value from our core belief system and working through what behaviours we would want to see that demonstrate this. Below are a couple of examples.

TABLE 4.1: Example behaviours and hats.

PRINCIPLES : Respect, Humility And Trust

PERSON	IDEAL BEHAVIOUR	ADAPTIVE LEADER HAT
Leader	Publicly recognise leaders and managers who lead with humility	Support
Manager	Pro-actively seek knowledge and improvement suggestions from their team	Coach
Front Line	Making sure everyone is included in team discussions and decisions	Coach / Support

It's not enough to just write down the behaviours. We see many organisations that spend a lot of time doing this, creating detailed launch plans and wonderful posters that quite quickly just become wallpaper. Leaders need to constantly lead by example in visibly living and breathing the behaviours. The behaviours need to be continuously reinforced in every meeting and every interaction.

Recognition focused on behaviours is critical. Rather than recognising people for achieving a particular goal, we need to recognise them for the behaviour they demonstrated to achieve that goal. Publicly recognising and thanking people for demonstrating a behaviour as soon as it happens is very powerful. Building discussion and acknowledgment of behaviours into every meeting agenda is also important.

And remember, we cannot ignore behaviours that are not aligned with respect, humility, and trust and must quickly call these out and deal with them.

One way to think about this is that as leaders we are gardeners of our culture. To maintain the desired culture, we must proactively manage the expected behaviours every day. We need to nurture and encourage the behaviours to thrive using recognition. We also need to deal quickly with any weeds (poor behaviours) or our culture will wither and die.

Recognition focused on behaviours is critical.

Once we have developed some behavioural expectations, we need to start measuring them using key behavioural indicators (KBIs). We will discuss how to develop and use these in more detail in chapter 10.

3 KEY TAKEAWAYS FROM THIS CHAPTER

1. Respect, humility, and trust are essential foundations for leading excellence.
2. We need to be clear on the behaviours that are expected in our organisation that demonstrate respect, humility, and trust.
3. We need to lead by example in demonstrating these behaviours and constantly manage and reinforce them through recognition

ACTIVITY 4: DEVELOPING BEHAVIOURAL EXPECTATIONS

In the introduction, we discussed an exercise around behaviours starting with how we want our frontline people and teams to behave and then working back up through to the leadership team.

1. To begin, select a principle or value that's important to you and the organisation (this is a good exercise to do as a team).
2. Ask yourself what behaviour you would like to see in a front-line team member or team that would clearly demonstrate this principle or value. **TIP:** Remember a behaviour must have an action word - it's something we could see happening. A simple test if something is a behaviour is to ask: Could I video that?
3. Once you've agreed on this behaviour, describe what behaviour would be needed by managers to support this behaviour within the team.
4. Then ask yourself what behaviour you need to demonstrate to support these behaviours in the managers and team members.
5. Finally, reflect on which adaptive leadership hat(s) you need to wear to help you with that behaviour.

Here is a blank template for you to try for yourself or with some colleagues.

TABLE 4.2: Activity 4.

CHOOSE A PRINCIPLE :

PERSON	DESCRIBE THE IDEAL BEHAVIOURS	WHICH HAT(S) WOULD YOU CHOOSE
Leader		
Manager		
Front Line		

5

PERSONAL PURPOSE
Planting trees that you may never sit under the shade of

The fundamental role of a great leader is to truly understand each person within their team. Thinking back to the core belief system model discussed in chapter 3, every individual has their own discrete beliefs, values, and behaviours. What influences these personal attributes is the individual's purpose. A great leader finds a way to connect the individual's purpose to the overall organisational purpose. When you connect the two, you unleash a level of engagement and performance that you could have only dreamed of previously. We often get asked the question: can you change a person's values, beliefs, or behaviours? The answer is: always, but it can vary.

You can change someone's behaviours by connecting them to a higher purpose and by developing systems that will drive ideal behaviours. People's behaviours are generally driven by internal and external factors that influence them. We will discuss how people's behaviours are impacted by internal and external factors in a bit more depth in chapter 8.

> Leaders who serve and focus their attention on understanding every team member's values and beliefs will have a greater level of success.

While you can change a person's values through experience and coaching, changing a person's beliefs usually requires an event that fundamentally alters that person's outlook or perception of life. This would have been experienced, for example, through the COVID-19 pandemic, where government policies and fear, in some instances, changed people's beliefs.

Leaders who serve and focus their attention on understanding every team member's values and beliefs will have a greater level of success over time. Through wearing the different leadership hats, a leader can get to understand people at a much deeper level. Understanding the characteristics of the different hats and knowing what each hat can contribute in particular circumstances is what creates an adaptive leader.

In today's world of volatility, uncertainty, complexity, and ambiguity (VUCA), a successful leader needs to adapt to the ever-changing environment to ensure that their people are always at the forefront of their minds.

You often hear sayings that ring true in so many ways such as this one widely attributed to Mahatma Gandhi:

> The sign of a good leader is not how many followers you have, it's how many leaders you create.

The fundamental role of any great leader is to see the true potential of every individual. Seeing people's true potential and devising systems to develop that person to be the best they can be so they can bring their whole, authentic selves to work each day creates an environment of trust, respect, and overall sustainable high performance.

Having a sixth sense for people's development and nurturing their aspirations and goals is the cornerstone of any leadership journey. Yet, most organisations fail to recognise that leadership takes years of personal and professional development. It takes years of failing, learning, adapting, and resilience to be able to lead teams through the many peaks, troughs, and challenges that they face.

No matter whether you're in a corporate role, a non-profit role, or a sporting role, as a leader, you need to work hard to develop others. You must have a deep sense of humility to realise that, one day, the leaders you create today will go on to be better than you will ever dream of being. That is the greatest satisfaction—the knowledge that you have influenced in some way, shape, or form the lives of one, or many. You have touched the lives of not only that future leader but also the lives of their families for generations to come. The reality is that you have created a legacy. You have planted a tree that has grown so strong it can withstand the ferocity of the changing environments, and its leaves have touched hundreds, if not thousands, of other lives.

I recall a few years back when speaking with a good friend they were talking about creating a legacy. What he said had a profound impact on the way I viewed my contribution to society as a leader: leadership is not a right; it's a privilege. It's a privilege to be able to impact so many people's lives positively.

There was a sombre moment, as he then described walking through a tree-filled cemetery one day, observing the many epitaphs. He reflected on one that simply read:

Robert Johnson
Touched the lives of many.
1918–1967

What stood out was not the name, the dates, or even the statement; it was the hyphen. I was baffled about where this was heading. The friend went on to explain, 'That hyphen defines you as a person, you choose your path, you choose where you want to go in life and what you wish to be remembered by. The hyphen is a symbol of your legacy.'

I spent days, if not weeks, pondering on that moment. What was my hyphen going to be? What would be the legacy that I would be remembered by?

> The people in your team or your organisation are the only asset that has the infinite capacity to appreciate in value.

A leader can impact the lives of many. The people in your team or your organisation are the only asset that has the infinite capacity to appreciate in value. A great leader recognises that and works hard to develop strong colleague and developmental systems.

COLLEAGUE ONBOARDING SYSTEMS

In 2019, I was fortunate to have the opportunity to lead a contact centre for one of the largest financial services banks in Australia. Contact centres are generally the poor cousin of any organisation; certainly, that is the way they are mostly viewed by senior leadership teams. They are the 'back office' staff who are entry-level. They tend to be seen as a division that has a high staff turnover, has a high unplanned sick leave, is generally managed to tight adherence schedules, and is expected to provide excellent service to the organisation's customer base.

I felt that this was the heartbeat of the organisation. This part of the business spoke to the highest number of customers in a day than any other department. It touched the lives of thousands of customers daily. Yet so many contact centres are treated as lower down the food chain of the organisation.

To me, it was the complete opposite. I had the opportunity to impact first on the lives of the 300+ colleagues and leaders who worked there. If I could develop the colleagues and leaders to be the best they can be, they in turn, would provide the best level of service to their large customer base daily.

When I first arrived, however, I noticed that the leaders, who were 28 in total, were spending an enormous amount of their time each week managing performance. We would never achieve our aspirations as a business if our leader's time was spent managing people rather than developing people. I needed to unpack this more.

After holding several problem-solving workshops,we got to the root cause of the problem. We were recruiting on technical ability and not taking into consideration character or behaviours in our assessments. We wanted colleagues to 'hit the ground running', to fill the seat as quickly as possible to avoid as much downtime as possible.

Yet this was counterproductive because what was happening was that some of the people who were being employed, whilst having the technical ability, lacked the ideal behaviours that were going to enable the business deliver on the team's vision.

The leadership team immediately went to work on designing the outcome that we wanted. We had already set a vision for the team, which was an aspirational target of a 'global best in class 'contact centre. With a broad selection of frontline colleagues, the team created the ideal behaviours we wanted to aspire to across all levels of the division. From frontline to team leaders to senior leaders to the Head of the Department we wanted a set of ideal behaviours that we could live by. We wanted a culture that gave our frontline teams the confidence to speak up and challenge those whose actions that were not meeting the agreed ideal behaviours.

Once we had agreed on the ideal behaviours, we then went and looked at the colleague onboarding system. We put on our support hats and changed our recruiting criteria away from technical ability and toward behaviour and character onboarding assessments.

We would have our leaders attend onboarding assessment centres to identify colleagues who best fit our company values and, more importantly, displayed the ideal behaviours we had mapped out. We even went as far as having some of the frontline colleagues at the assessment centres select their peers that 'they wanted on their team'.

This ensured that anyone coming through the assessment centres had the right character and behaviours aligned with our values and our new vision to be global best in class.

It took time for the leadership teams to work through the high number of HR performance improvement cases we had when I first took over. Some underperforming colleagues managed to turn around, some didn't, and we had to make the tough calls to let them go as they were not the right fit to move the business forward.

We have experienced many businesses over our expansive careers where we have seen inappropriate leadership behaviours when managing poor performance or behaviours. Whilst moving the problem to another division or team is a short-term leadership win, it is a poor decision for the organisation. As a leader, you need to hold people to account for poor behaviours. If you do not, you will quickly destroy your culture.

Once we changed the recruitment system to being one based on ideal behaviours and character assessments, it was like a game of two halves. Suddenly, the time spent on managing performance and wearing the direct hat dropped considerably and time spent on development systems and wearing our support, coach, and teach hats rose.

The leadership team created an onboarding system where we identified every new employee's aspiration. Some had goals to be in finance, some in change management, some in communications, product development, and many more. We identified that there were more than 240 different career pathways across the group of companies. After identifying each new employee's aspirations, the leaders then donned their support, coach, and teach hats and created a development pathway with key actions and milestones for each employee to achieve their true potential. We designed a visual career pathway map and explained to every employee in their first week in the business where they could go and what they needed to do to get there.

This early discussion was personally enlightening. We built into the onboarding system a leadership standard work process that on day 1 the senior leadership team and I would wear our inspire hats and spend time with the new recruits. We would introduce ourselves personally, and explain to them their career pathways, and the culture that had been created so that all employees could come to work each day feeling safe and their voices were as loud as any other.

Day 1 was always my favourite, as I could see the light in people's eyes when they explained their development pathways. They weren't just joining the contact centre; they had the infinite capacity to grow into their true potential by choosing from over 240 different roles. They felt a part of something much bigger. They were energised from day 1.

We created a new training system also that reduced our 'time to live', which was the term for the time it took to get them working on the phones taking calls. Previously, it took 8 weeks of classroom time to get them to a level of competency; however, this new system was 'learn by doing' as people learn much faster than in traditional classroom-style training. This new training system meant our 'time to live' went from eight weeks to two weeks. At the end of week two, they were taking their first calls. The leadership team built a strong coaching system to support these new employees which developed them through the required capability tiers to enable them to perform their roles to the required standards.

LEADER STANDARD WORK

The leader standard work rhythm, created within the onboarding system, included another senior leadership touch point at the end of induction training. This was when new employees got a deeper understanding of the organisation's culture of continuous improvement. The leaders put on their teach hats and introduced them to the basic tools that the frontline teams used to solve problems, such as:

- Identifying and designing a problem statement.
- Fishbone—cause and effect.
- 5-Whys.
- P.I.C.K solution selection matrix.

Keeping it simple and providing the frontline teams with the tools to problem solve themselves helps create a culture of every team member, everywhere, solving problems every day. This was a business that was challenging to be able to 'take people off the tools' to do continuous improvement. Like many other businesses running a tight adherence to schedules and workforce planning systems, you can't just take people off the tools and expect the performance of the business not to be affected. However, if you want the ideal behaviour of everybody, everywhere, improving your business by 1% every day, then you need to create a system that will drive that behaviour.

> Create a culture of every team member, everywhere, solving problems every day.

A system that works well in a capacity constraint environment such as contact centres or mining production, or maintenance is what called an *improvement champion system*.

Let's take a deeper look into this system and how it works.

IMPROVEMENT CHAMPION SYSTEM

The leader of each team selects one frontline colleague to be the improvement champion for that team. This individual has dedicated time each week to work on improvement opportunities that the team has identified through deviations in their operating performance boards or visual management boards. The champions come together for 90 minutes or more each week to solve these problems individually and collectively under the coaching of the business improvement team. They work collectively across teams to solve cross-functional/cross-team problems or work individually on solving problems within their own control.

They have a weekly problem-solving workshop that the senior leadership attends, and they provide updates on their progress. Some of which hit a roadblock. The role of the senior leadership is not to do the work for them when they hit this roadblock. It's to use the coach and support hats and remove that roadblock and assist them in navigating the senior stakeholder group in opening doors for them so they can continue with their problem-solving. One of their key roles as improvement champions is also to work with their teams to inform them about what they are working on, their experience, and their learnings throughout their journey.

Generally, they are in the champion program for 3 to 6 months where, at the end of their program, they present their portfolio of improvement opportunities to the senior leadership team. Some do just one problem-solving, some a few, depending on the original scope. They are then presented with a Yellow Belt in Continuous Improvement. The capacity they create through their improvements is reinvested to enable more colleagues the opportunity to become improvement champions and learn how to problem-solve.

They then return to their teams after their 3- to 6-month term; however, they still have dedicated time each week to continue with their problem-solving journey. A new champion is then selected for the next 3- to 6-month program.

With this system in place, over time you drive the behaviour of having everybody across your business or team solving problems each day. The system drives the behaviour of having every individual off the tools each week for problem-solving; something you envisioned at the start of the journey yet deemed impossible in a capacity-constrained environment.

The impossible can be achieved with the right systems in place. Focus on the behaviour you want then design the system that will get you that behaviour. Of course, the design of the

> The impossible can be achieved with the right systems in place.

system cannot be in isolation. A system or process is only as good as its supporting systems or processes. In this regard, to drive a highly engaged system of problem solvers, solving problems everywhere, every day, you need to create a reward and recognition system to underpin it.

With reward and recognition systems, it's less about the reward and more about the recognition. Colleagues love to be recognised for their hard work or values-driven ideal behaviours. A leader can have a profound impact on a colleague's performance just by merely acknowledging them for the job they are doing. People feel heard, accepted, and energised.

The system mentioned earlier had the reward of the yellow belt presentation; however, it was the regular repetition of the leaders linking what people were doing back to the organisation's purpose and vision to be global best in class that made the difference. They felt connected. They felt they were contributing to the vision.

The creation of a continuous improvement (CI) of the month award was another way of recognising the great work the frontline team was doing. Getting their CI award and their photo on the CI wall of fame made them feel connected and empowered. They are simple systems that drive huge engagement, customer, colleague, and business outcomes.

DEVELOPING LEADER TALENT
(Coach and Teach Hats)

In typical command- and-control type organisations or teams, leaders lead with no concept of developing the organisations future talent. They are protective of their own roles and fearful of developing people beyond their own leadership capabilities. While these leaders do get results, they may not achieve ideal results.

The word *ideal* is so important. Ideal means results that are sustained over time. They are results that don't waver or depend on individual leaders being present. The results continue to improve year on year, regardless of internal or external interferences. Sure, a hubris leader will get spot results. They may achieve their own personal goals if they hit a 2- or 3-year strategic metric and move on to other roles or organisations.

Meanwhile, the culture that they have left behind is one of disengagement, high unplanned sick leave, and high attrition. On the other hand, if you have a leader who leads with humility and focuses their long-term strategic goals on creating strong development systems for their leaders and frontline teams, you create long-term sustainable results well beyond the 3- or 5-year horizons.

Many organisations coach and mentor leaders to be good managers. They coach them to do leader-standard work well in parts; leadership skills such as how to run an effective one-to-one or how to have a development conversation. While these are good things to know and learn, they fundamentally miss the underlying opportunity to create and develop adaptive leaders who think systemically.

Let's take the one-to-one discussion as an example.

We coach our leaders to meet with their teams once a week or month to go through the standard questions:

1. In the last month, what has gone well?
2. What could you have done better?
3. Development plan actions and how you are progressing?
4. What support do you need from your leader?

So, the leader and the team member go through the motions and part company for another week or month until the next discussion. We are teaching our leaders to be people managers, not people leaders. We are effectively going through the motions because it's the accepted thing to do in the corporate world.

This means that we are sending our people back onto the frontline to work in a system that has a sizeable amount of waste built into their processes. Some organisations or divisions we have observed have people working in systems with upwards of 70% waste in them. They are working within processes that are cumbersome, with many handoffs, reworks, signoffs, and even better, quality assurance checks (QA).

The latter, for example, is one that still baffles us to this day. How often do we see organisations build quality assurance teams to check the work? Sometimes checking it two or three times. They spend hundreds of thousands if not millions each year checking quality after the work has been completed. The defect is already in the product or service by the time it's inspected, so why place so much emphasis on QA?

> Leaders should spend their time coaching their teams to identify improvement opportunities and solve problems.

If you divert a fraction of your QA resources to the front end and help people to get it right at the time of production, you will reduce your defect rate considerably and remove the requirement to have an extensive QA expense at the back end, where it adds no value to the customer.

What we should be doing instead is using our coach hat to coach our leaders to be system leaders. They should spend more time with their teams going to *Look, Listen and Learn* the defective systems their teams are working in. The term *Look, Listen and Learn* means to go to where the work is performed, as that's where you will find the problems and the solutions. Leaders should spend their time coaching their teams to identify improvement opportunities and solve problems in the processes they perform each day.

When leaders *Look, Listen and Learn* with a purpose and coach their teams to identify and solve problems at the root cause the frontline starts to feel heard and supported. They feel connected to the organisation's purpose or vision. They feel empowered to effect change. They are no longer doing mundane tasks. They are ideating, creating, and developing new and better ways of doing things. They feel energised to come to work each day because they feel that they are contributing to making the business better today than it was yesterday. The term *Look, Listen and Learn* will be explored in more detail later in chapter 10.

Similarly, most organisations have robust performance review systems in place that leaders must spend countless hours preparing, conducting, and administering. Some organisations require these to be done by leaders every quarter. Yet again, leaders are focusing their time on the things that don't necessarily drive the right behaviours or outcomes.

One-to-ones and performance reviews can be seen as reactive, lagging systems in any organisation if they are not performed correctly. Done right, the leader would interchange between the coach and teach hats to use these routines to help the employees improve the processes they are working in. They should be creating the environment where every individual comes to work each day bringing their whole selves, ideating, and challenging the standards. We often set standards, create standard operating procedures, and insist that teams follow these standards. Yet we don't coach and develop them to challenge the standards. Just because it's the way we do it now doesn't mean there isn't an easier, better, faster, or cheaper way of doing things.

Another potential wasteful system if not used correctly is the standard half-yearly people engagement surveys. If this system is used just to check the engagement levels of employees without a strong improvement cycle to support it then it becomes non-value-added waste. That said, a strong leader knows how much their team is engaged and already has the right culture in their team to be action planning daily, not just when the engagement survey results come out. A system that has waste built into it will start to wear people down over time. They start to feel distracted from the organisation's purpose, which then leaves them disconnected and frustrated.

> We should be coaching leaders to identify the leading indicators of where culture is slipping.

A leader who is developed in systems thinking knows when the team needs to action plan ahead of time. They have daily and weekly routines with their teams where the team can identify deviations in performance. Their teams will feel safe to constructively challenge their peers and their leaders. They will look to continuously improve.

We should be coaching leaders to identify the leading indicators of where culture is slipping. What are the unplanned sick leave trends? What is attrition like and is that trending up or down? Is the productivity per person increasing or decreasing over time? Is overtime reducing? If overtime is present and/or increasing, this would be a leading indicator of ineffective systems in place. So, what are we coaching our leaders to do in these circumstances? What are the contingency plans to address these deviations in performance?

UNDERSTANDING TYPE AND FREQUENCY OF DEMAND

One of the great thought leaders on systems thinking, John Seddon from Vanguard Consulting articulates the two different types of demand in organisations quite eloquently, (first described in his book 'I want you to cheat' 1992). He maintains that understanding the type and frequency of demand in your organisation or team is also a critical skill of the systems leader. Every organisation, no matter what they produce or what service they provide, essentially has two types of demand (see Figure 5.1 below).

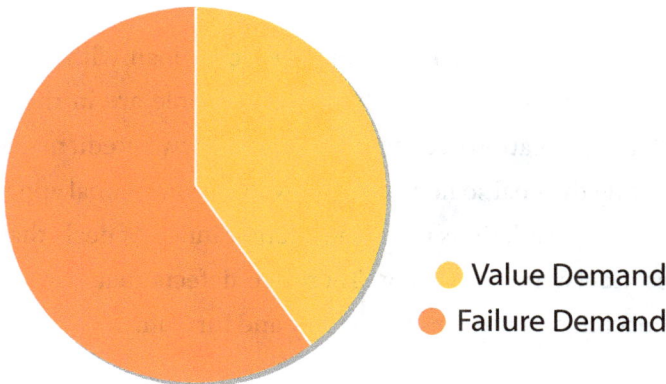

FIGURE 5.1: Value demand and failure demand (based on the work of John Seddon)

Value demand

Why the organisation exists. This is what the organisation is producing or the service that it is providing. In financial services, for example, this could be things like a home loan product that offers a redraw facility with unconditional approval in 24 hours. In the hospitality services industry, this could be things like a clean room with clean linen and tasty food. It's what the customer wants to *pull* from you. It's what the customer is prepared to pay you for.

Failure Demand

Failure demand is a failure to do what's right for the customer the first time. It's a failure to provide the level of service or product they specifically asked for. It's all the defects in your system—the reworks, unnecessary handoffs, the extensive approval processes, and the number of signatures required to fulfil the product or service. It's the work that customers are not prepared to pay for.

In the example of financial services and the home loan with a redraw facility, the customer doesn't care how many people are in the value chain or that the application needed to pass through two credit managers due to reworking the deal so hence the delay in unconditional approval, or the fact that the validations team had a larger influx of deals that day so there was a delay in processing. These are defects that our leaders need to be coaching their teams to identify and turn off.

When leaders coach and mentor teams to identify and delete failure demand, you increase your capacity to provide more value-added time to your customers. You start to balance your capacity and demand more effectively. You start to reduce the waste in your overall system. You start to create more capacity for leaders to do what they should be doing.

They should be spending 70-80% of their time in the field with their teams, wearing the coach and support hats, developing and helping their team members to identify and solve problems at the root cause.

Instead, leaders only coach team members by doing one-on-ones and performance reviews, which are reactive systems. No wonder they are spending 70%-80% on the system of work. They are reactive in nature. They are in firefighting mode, introducing band-aid solutions to try to balance all the plates they are spinning. They are working harder, later, and getting more stressed. Leaders are in the endless spinning wheel or vortex that they can't seem to get out of. They can't get out of it because traditional leader development is not focusing on the right things. Sound familiar?

By focusing on the ideal behaviours that you want to drive the outcomes that your business needs and then having your leaders build the systems that will drive that behaviour, you will achieve sustainable or ideal results.

CASE STUDY: SMALL BUSINESS DIVISION—FINANCIAL SERVICES BUSINESS IN AUSTRALIA

The senior leadership team of the Small Business (SB) Division struggled for years to get any growth in their Small Business Credit Card portfolio. Growth numbers were on the decline and customer satisfaction with the product was at an all-time low. The team engaged the services of one of their internal business improvement colleagues who was a Black Belt in Continuous Improvement to conduct an improvement project to understand the extent of the problem and ultimately solve the problem for the business.

The problem statement was easy to define, as limited sales and high turnaround time was driving customers to look elsewhere for their product. This heightened the risk of customer attrition to other banks as the SB credit card was seen as a key product to attract new customers.

Data collected in the preliminary stages of the project identified some alarming statistics. On average, it was taking 116 days from when a customer submitted an application to the customer having their card ordered. Quite a painful experience for customers, especially for that demographic of customers who rely heavily on cash flow.

Further investigations through *Look, Listen and Learn* observations on the frontline call team when customers called to request an SB credit card found that the staff had lost complete faith in the process and were actively advising customers to go elsewhere for the product. What they also found was that there was a considerable amount of documentation required for these customers. Most applications were from existing customers of the bank with an extensive credit and transactional history. The majority of lending limits on these cards was less than $10,000. There were also multiple handoffs to other stakeholders within the value stream and each one had its own service-level agreement. A perfect storm!

The project team gathered the stakeholders into a room and mapped on the wall every document in each stage of the process. Stakeholders included the heads of credit risk, regulatory risk, legal, and the small business executives. The team went to each document and asked the stakeholders the following questions:

1. Was this document a credit risk requirement to fulfil the needs of the credit application or can we rely on existing information held on the customer's profile to progress the deal?
2. Was this document a regulatory requirement?
3. Was there any legal requirement that we are not aware of that we need this document to protect the bank and or customer?
4. Or was it a process document?

What we meant by process document was, at some stage over the years, had an error or defect occurred in the process and someone had requested that a new document to be completed to 'make us feel a bit safer'.

Going around the room, stopping at each part of the process, and asking the above questions was quite alarming: over 80% of the documents on the wall were process documents. Over the years, leadership had added more complexity to the process without truly understanding the impact on the customer or had relied on an extra document when, really, they could have used the existing transactional data history of the customer to progress the deal. The project team then agreed with each stakeholder whether to remove each process document from the application process.

The next stage of the project was to address the remaining points of failure demand—the excessive handoffs. When teams work in a functional design organisation that doesn't create flow in their processing, they generally design failure demand systems such as Service Level Agreements (SLA). Each part of the value stream has independent SLAs that they need to meet each day to hit their targets. These targets are arbitrary as they add no value to the customer.

We see this all the time in organisations. Instead of case management, we create defective systems such as queue management: we push the customer into different queues; meanwhile, the teams are meeting their KPIs, yet the customer is waiting in the queue. Anywhere there are SLAs in place in the service industry should be a red flag that could potentially impact your customer experience.

In this case, applications spent 24 hours in the validations queue before being actioned. Once the deal was picked up, it was validated. If there was a piece of information missing, the validator would put it back in the queue for the frontline to follow up with the customer. As far as the validator was concerned, they had met their daily target so they were all content.

The frontline colleague would then contact the customer, collect the missing piece of information, and then resubmit the application into the validations queue for another 24-hour SLA. If validated, it would then be sent to the credit manager queue, which had a 48-hour SLA. If they required more information, it was sent back to the frontline again to repeat the process.

You can see where this is going and why it took 116 days to fulfil the customer's needs. Meanwhile, each team was meeting their KPI because they were all within their arbitrary target SLA.

What the project team did next was not that revolutionary. They created a test and learn process and arranged for those in the value stream to sit together in a U-shaped pod, similar to that in the manufacturing industry. They created a flow of customer cases and closed off the queue system completely.

Instead, the project team got the people in the value stream to speak to each other rather than placing customers into a queue. If a customer's application was missing a piece of information, the validator reached across and spoke to the credit manager and collectively discussed the deal and the existing transactional history of the customer. If they still needed more information, they simply phoned the customer directly.

They case owned each deal through to card ordering. Turnaround time dropped from 116 days to 3.4 days without any technology improvements. This is a simple example of understanding failure demand and turning it off.

This team then started to feel more connected to the organisation's purpose. They felt that they were able to deliver on what customers valued. They felt an enormous amount of pride in the fact that they could assist their customers in meeting their financial needs and felt empowered to make decisions to progress customer cases. They were now being adaptive to meeting different customer's needs. The leaders in that area were using all the leadership hats to help their teams improve the system. Coaching leaders to be adaptive, use different hats, and think this way will transform the way your organisation operates and ultimately improve your customers' experience.

3 KEY TAKEAWAYS FROM THIS CHAPTER:

1. Identify waste in your processes and coach your teams to use problem-solving tools to help remove failure demand so you focus more on what your customers value.

2. Focus your teams on recruiting for ideal behaviours and character over technical ability.

3. Spend some personal time reflecting on what your legacy will be as a leader. What do you want to be remembered for?

ACTIVITY 5

TABLE 5.1: Activity 5

ACTION	IDEAL BEHAVIOUR	ADAPTIVE LEADER HAT(S)
Select one of your direct reports and at your next scheduled one-to-one discussion, instead of doing the standard discussion, go on a Look Listen and Learn Walk on one of the key processes they perform each day and go with the specific purpose to identify one improvement to that process. Think of the following: How can we make this, Easier, Better, Faster or Cheaper (in that order)?	Leaders are seeking to understand the improvement opportunities in processes that their teams are working on.	Inspire Support Teach Coach

6

PERSONAL PURPOSE
Nurturing the trees

In chapter 5 we discussed the importance of focusing on recruiting for ideal behaviours and character over technical ability. In this chapter we will explore how to continuously develop and grow your leader talent with the right mindsets and behaviours. Now that we have identified that leaders need to understand the different types of demand in any organisation and inspire them to create their own legacy, we now need to turn our attention to how we can grow our leader talent with the right mindsets and behaviours. To drive the desired outcome of developing leadership talent that ensures the sustainability of performance, we need

> We need to create a leader talent system.

to create a leader talent system. This is a simple development system that has been used for years and is one that is extremely effective in ensuring that leaders have the right coaching and development actions in place to advance through their careers within your organisation. This system will also assist in retaining your high performing individuals and reduce the risk of leader attrition.

Further, it's a system that will deeply connect individual team purpose to the organisational purpose. Sometimes when you use this system to its true extent, you can identify a gap between someone's personal purpose and the organisational purpose. When a misalignment appears, the leader must then switch to the coach hat to truly understand where that individual's full potential lies.

We have had a few instances over the years where exactly this has occurred. We spent time to understand what drove the individual and what was their personal purpose. On some occasions, that meant finding them another role in the organisation and some have meant the individual has left the organisation and gone onto another industry where they fulfilled their personal purpose. This generally can be identified through this model in the *need a change of role* category which we will discuss below.

Firstly, you need to create a standard routine or meeting. This can be monthly; however, the suggestion is to do it quarterly so you can start to see movement in the talent cycle. The routine is for your leadership team to get together and talk to the individual leaders in their respective teams. You can also use this matrix at all levels of your organisation. Let's look at the model in a bit more detail (see Figure 6.1 below).

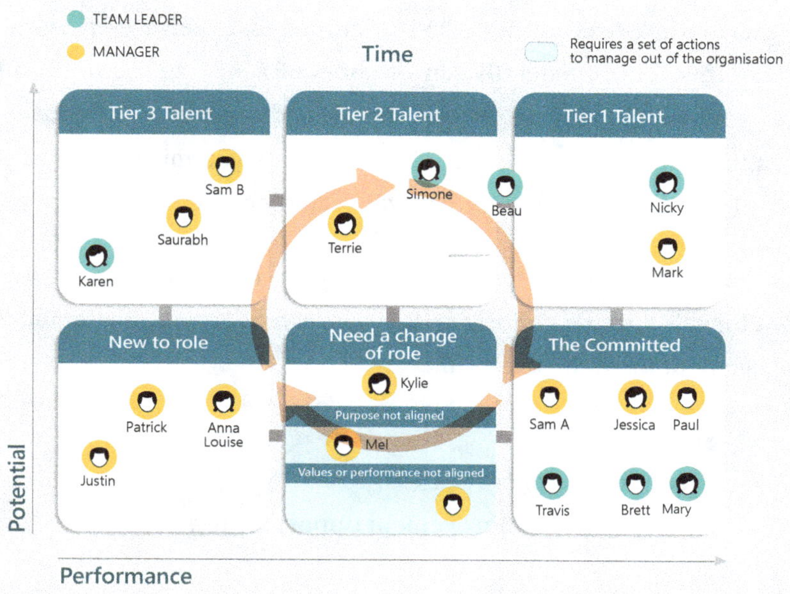

FIGURE 6.1: Leader talent assessment matrix.

LEADER TALENT ASSESSMENT MATRIX

The committed

These are the colleagues in your organisation you can't do without. They are the backbone of your operation. They are the people who have limited or no interest in career progression. They come to work each day to give 100% and they're happy to be part of the team. They don't want for much.

However, leaders need to be cognisant of the need to keep them engaged. They need to find ways to ensure that they are energised at work. This cohort generally can be about 60% of your team. If leaders ignore these employees, they'll become disengaged and leave the organisation. Therefore, as a leadership group, you must agree on your routines and specific actions that will keep them focused.

We like to use the term *engagement plan* rather than *development plan* for this specific cohort. Things that can be used to maintain their engagement might be things like:

- Specific projects.
- Secondments to other areas.
- Involvement in improvement opportunities.
- Subject matter experts.
- Advisory on process areas.
- Assisting with the design of new standards or processes.

New to role

This component includes those colleagues or leaders whom it is too soon to rate because they are new to the role or the organisation. They have been in the role for less than 12 months so there hasn't been enough demonstration of their capabilities or behaviours to warrant any specific change to their development planning.

The focus for this group should be ensuring that they have been onboarded effectively. Their leaders wear the support, teach, and coach hats and they are given the correct tools of trade to enable them to be effective in their roles. They have the appropriate coaching and training to get them role fit.

Need a change of role

This is where the colleague or leader has been in a role for an extended period e.g. three to five or more years. Often, if an individual is in a role for an extended length of time, they run the risk of role fatigue. They become stagnant. They lose the ability to see opportunities for improvement and generally their energy levels start to diminish.

These are generally people who are values-driven and display the expected ideal behaviours. They have just reached a standstill in the role. A new role in another team or function that aligns with their personal purpose would reignite them. It would give them a new sense of purpose and energise them.

The need a change of role component is also broken down into two further actionable categories:

Purpose not aligned

As previously mentioned in chapter 5, connecting an individual's personal purpose to a higher organisational purpose drives a level of engagement and performance you could only dream of previously. Sometimes, though, an individual may not be performing or may be displaying poor behaviours because their purpose is not aligned to the organisation.

In these scenarios, the leader needs to switch hats to coach the individual to see the true pathway they should be taking. This is often a role that is outside the organisation and one that connects to the individual's purpose. A very left-field example of this could be the individual's purpose is aligned to strong environmental protection and ensuring that commercialism doesn't impact the natural landscape, yet they work for a mining company or oil and gas.

Values or performance not aligned

This category of the model is related to employee performance and whether they are meeting the organisation's expectations. This can include either underperforming from a business outcomes perspective or not meeting the required company values, code of conduct, or the ideal behaviours you would expect in your organisation. A misalignment in this part of the model can cause irreparable damage to the culture of the organisation if not managed effectively.

> As leaders, you need to understand that individual's personal circumstances and support them through whatever those interferences may be.

Some colleagues or leaders may be underperforming because of internal or external interferences impacting their ability to consistently perform to a high level. We will speak more about the impacts that interferences have on a high performing individual later in chapter 8.

As leaders, you need to understand that individual's personal circumstances and support them through whatever those interferences may be. Assisting them to navigate that, wearing the coach hat and taking them through an effective coaching plan, can really turn an individual's performance around.

However, what we often see in organisations is leaders not managing or holding to account those whose performance is poor or who are displaying poor behaviours. How you treat an individual impacts on the many.

On the one hand, not holding poor-performing colleagues to account will diminish your culture in a matter of months. You will see high-performing colleagues start to become disengaged.

On the other hand, there are also organisations where leaders are not managing the underperformance by pushing that problem onto another team or function to manage. This is also a form of poor behaviour by the leader. This is a culture you will see in many organisations and one that has a profound effect on the outcomes of the culture and performance of the organisation.

Tier 3 talent

The tier 3 category of individuals includes those who continually display the ideal behaviours and perform to a very high standard over time. They come to work each day, energised to effect change. They continually go the extra mile to help their teams and others with tasks. They are the first to offer help. They are humble and will roll up their sleeves at a moment's notice.

You need these people in your organisation to drive the energy and strategy forward. These are your doers and the people who are the spearhead of your arrow. Generally, these people have been consistently high performing for a period of 12-24 months.

The leadership group needs to ensure that there are strong development actions for this cohort to keep them motivated and engaged. You need to ensure that their reward and recognition system is adequate to fulfil their needs and continually recognise them for their efforts and outcomes.

Tier 2 talent

These are colleagues who have been moved from the Tier 3 Talent category and are deemed by the leadership group to be ready for a promotion in 18 months or more. These are your potential aspiring leaders coming through the matrix. This cohort generally has a more advanced level of development around leadership.

Their leaders work with them to uplift their capabilities in leadership fundamentals. Ideally, they work with them to develop them into enterprise leaders who lead with humility. They are aspiring leaders who work collectively to solve business problems. They get opportunities to go on secondments into other areas to cover for existing leaders who may be on leave or some form of career break from the organisation.

Tier 1 talent

This cohort is your second in command, your next generation of leaders, and are generally ready for promotion within the next 12 months. These are the people who run your business when you are not around. They are the ones who can step in and take over at a moment's notice. Again, their level of development is the highest. They get extended levels of development coaching and organisational leadership training and are seconded cross-functionally to ensure they get exposure across the organisation.

As the leadership team conduct your talent routines, the team speaks to every individual in this tier and provides updates on each development action, progress to their plans, and outcomes they are delivering. The idea is that, over time, each person moves clockwise through the grid as defined by the orange arrow. If individuals are not moving through the grid, then the discussion is around why not—what are the roadblocks and what specific actions the leadership group needs to take to address that gap in movement. This is an effective tool to ensure you develop your leaders with the right level of support and coaching.

ASPIRING LEADERS DEVELOPMENT SYSTEM

As mentioned previously, aspiring leaders are your grassroots leaders who need to be nurtured. If you want to build strong leader talent across your organisation, focusing on developing an effective aspiring leader's development system will you ensure that you are creating a pipeline of leaders who have the ideal behaviours and values that will support the organisation's vision and purpose. You will create leaders who are culturally aligned. Their core belief system will align to the organisation's, which in turn drives more high performing, sustainable results.

> A strong aspiring leader program can have a wide range of benefits for organisations.

A strong aspiring leader program can have a wide range of benefits for organisations, including increased employee engagement, improved leadership skills, and enhanced organisational performance. In this book, we will explore these benefits in more detail and discuss how a strong aspiring leader program can help organisations achieve their goals.

1. **Increased employee engagement:** One of the primary benefits of a strong aspiring leader program is increased employee engagement. Having leaders who serve their teams create strong development systems that ultimately improve employee engagement. When employees see that their organisation is investing in their professional development and offering them opportunities to grow and advance, they are more likely to feel valued and connected to the organisation. This can lead to higher levels of motivation and job satisfaction, which can in turn increase productivity and reduce turnover.

2. **Improved leadership skills:** A strong aspiring leader program can help develop and improve the leadership skills of participants. Through training, coaching, and mentoring, aspiring leaders can learn how to communicate effectively, manage teams, make strategic decisions, and inspire others. These skills can benefit not only the individual but also their team and the whole organisation.

3. **Enhanced organisational performance:** By developing the leadership skills of aspiring leaders, organisations can enhance their overall performance. Effective leaders can help create a positive work environment, improve collaboration and teamwork, and drive innovation and growth. They can also help ensure that the organisation is aligned with its goals and mission and that resources are being used effectively.

4. **Succession planning:** A strong aspiring leader program can play a crucial role in succession planning. By identifying and developing potential leaders, organisations can ensure a smooth transition of leadership when current leaders retire or move on. This can help

minimize disruption to the organisation and ensure continuity of operations.

5. **Competitive advantage:** Finally, a strong aspiring leader program can provide organisations with a competitive advantage. By developing a pipeline of talented leaders, organisations can stay ahead of the competition and adapt to changing market conditions. They can also attract and retain high performing individuals by offering opportunities for growth and advancement.

While working with many organisations across the globe, we have seen many that struggle to develop their leadership talent from the grassroots level. They often find themselves in situations where a leadership role comes up and they need to either advertise externally because there is no capability inhouse or they look to backfill the role internally with a new leader who has not been set up for success and hasn't had the fundamental training and coaching a new leader needs to be able to perform their roles effectively. They are expected to hit the ground running, to suddenly adapt to being a new leader in an organisation, taking on the responsibility of their team and their team's performance. These organisations have failed these new leaders from the outset.

The system creates leaders with the right ideal behaviours, centred around humility, respect, and trust.

Let's take a close look at an example of an aspiring leaders development system that you could adopt. This system can be extremely effective in building a pipeline of talent which can be used to feed the organisation's future leaders. The system creates leaders with the right ideal behaviours, centred around humility, respect, and trust. It creates leaders who have systems thinking and who are already focused on their people and ideal behaviours.

One company that implemented this system had great results. In its first year of implementation, 75% of a 22-strong cohort were successful in obtaining a leadership role, with that number rising to 100% in the following year.

The business sent out expressions of interest each year for colleagues who had leadership as part of their career aspirations. These were mainly frontline colleagues who wanted to develop into leadership roles.

The development system is a year-long program that had six stages of theory development supported by a dedicated mentor. Mentors should be selected from across the organisation to balance the development needs of each delegate.

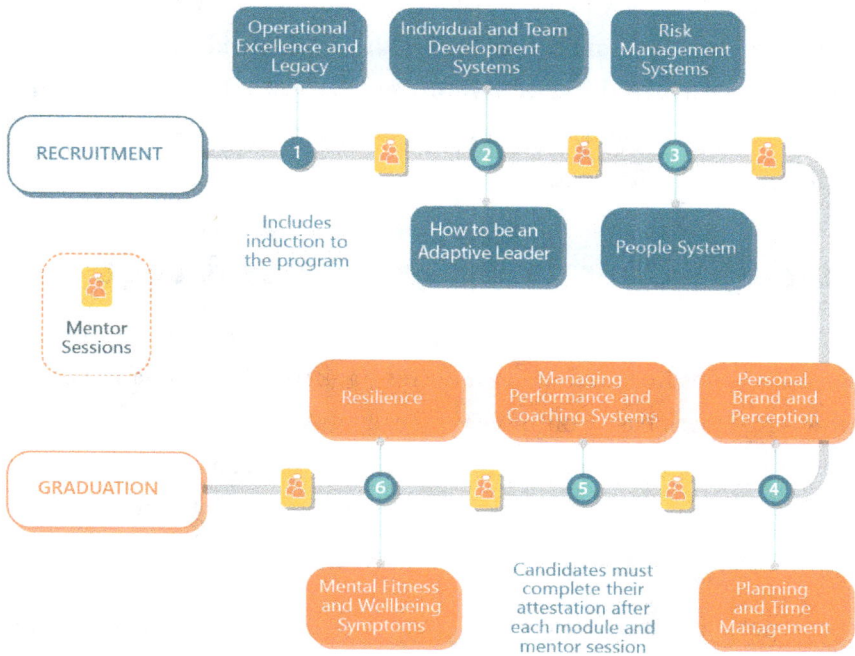

FIGURE 6.2: Aspiring leaders development system.

Pre-stage—Recruitment

As mentioned above, the leadership team communicated across the organisation looking for expressions of interest to join the leadership program. Candidates would go through an interview process to assess their career aspirations, their individual development areas, and, more importantly, their 'why' they wanted to become a leader.

This latter part was of the utmost importance. They needed to find colleagues who wanted to be a leader to serve a higher purpose, not ones who were chasing the title or the money. They wanted colleagues to go to where they are most alive and tingling at work so as to ensure they could replicate that many times over in their role as a leader. They wanted candidates who are passionate about developing their people to be the best they can be, who lead with humility and have respect for each person. Once the selection process was completed, the aspiring leaders cohort would then be locked into a year-long, 6-stage process, with a mentor assigned to each one.

Stage 1—Operational Excellence & Legacy

Once the candidates were selected for the program, each was given a book by James Kerr, called *Legacy*. This book was the foundation of the program. It was based on the New Zealand All Black's 15 practices of leadership that ensured they held the highest standards of sustainable performance and got them to be the number 1 rugby union team in the world.

Each delegate was instructed to pre-read the book prior to the commencement of stage 1 of the pathway. In the opening workshop, they would go through each of the leadership practices in a detailed breakout discussion. This session would then be followed by an introduction to Shigeo Shingo and the Shingo Model. The candidates would then be taken through the three Shingo Insights:

1. Ideal results require ideal behaviours.
2. Purpose and systems drive behaviours.
3. Principles inform ideal behaviours.

They would then go through each of the three dimensions and 10 principles in more detail.

Mentor session

At the end of each workshop, the candidates would be given homework to practice what they had learned in the staged workshop. Their mentors would also be given the candidate's homework and what they needed to do, so that when they met up with their candidate they could go through what they had learned with them, challenge them on their mindsets, and hold them accountable for achieving each milestone. They and their mentor would be then required to sign off on each module and their learnings. This process ensured that each delegate and mentor were comfortable for them to proceed to the next stage of development.

Stage 2—Individual and team development systems

The organisation had a big focus on people development. One of the key roles of their leaders was to create leaders who focused on building and improving systems that helped to shape the ideal behaviours required to achieve the company's vision. Quite often, when we recruit leaders, we don't provide them with the foundations of leadership to help them be proficient in their roles. This system helped provide the aspiring leaders with a basic level of knowledge and understanding of what makes a great leader.

Stage 2 was developed to walk each aspiring leader through all of the organisation's existing development systems to enable them to coach and mentor their teams more effectively, from how to conduct an effective one-to-one development conversation to defining and cascading developing pathways for their teams. Each candidate was provided with the required tools and systems and guidance on how and when to use each of these so that they could be more effective in driving the right outcomes for their teams.

How to be an adaptive leader

Stage 2 also took the candidates through some of the concepts that we speak about in this book. Aspiring leaders were coached on which hat they need to wear in which circumstance. Having one leadership approach wouldn't set them up for success, so the concept of wearing different hats was introduced to get them accustomed to thinking and acting differently in a variety of scenarios.

Stage 3—Risk management systems

In all organisations, risk management is one of the most critical components of an effective leader. Yet, when we recruit leaders, we expect them to be proficient in risk management without any training and then wonder why they struggle to grasp the sheer criticality of that component of their roles.

Stage 3 was developed to give aspiring leaders a foundation in risk, key compensating controls, key process management, and risk-in-change systems. The latter is where most organisations either fail to recognise or fail to invest in any meaningful system that helps their people absorb and understand change.

As mentioned earlier, we are living in a world of VUCA. Change is a constant. From new product development and new product features to mandatory learning and increased regulatory scrutiny, we are asking our people to increasingly take on more change each day. Most organisations don't see the value in a management-of-change system. This stage gave them not only a clear understanding of their roles in risk management but also a deeper understanding of their role in change management.

People system

Most corporate institutions have some sort of enterprise agreement. An enterprise agreement is made at the enterprise level and contains terms and conditions of employment, including wages, for a period of up to 4 years from the date of approval. Understanding this agreement in detail helps new leaders protect the institution and the rights of each employee covered by the agreement.

Stage 3 provides aspiring leaders with the knowledge and understanding of how to ensure that each of their teams covered by the agreement gets what they are entitled to under that said agreement. It also gives them the knowledge and processes that a leader would need to follow when dealing with unions to ensure that they are not putting their team or the organisation at risk.

The team were also introduced to standard corporate people systems, such as:

- Performance management.
- Development planning.
- Recruitment and onboarding.
- Offboarding.
- Coaching systems and frameworks.

Stage 4—Personal brand and perception

Personal brand and perception are critical for a leader in an organisation for several reasons. A leader's personal brand represents how they are perceived by colleagues, employees, customers, and stakeholders. It is, essentially, the sum of the leader's skills, experience, reputation, and personality traits that make them stand out from others. Perception, on the other hand, is how others view the leader's personal brand.

Yet we don't coach our leaders on how to build and nurture their personal brand in an organisation. What they are perceived to be can have a dramatic impact on their future career pathways and successes in any organisation.

> Learning how to use different hats in a variety of circumstances will greatly assist the leader to become an adaptive leader.

Perception can be influenced by a wide range of factors, such as communication style, behaviour, and track record. This is such an important lesson for any leader who is looking to build on their leadership capabilities. Learning how to use different hats in a variety of circumstances will greatly assist the leader to become an adaptive leader. They will no longer be pigeonholed into one type of hat. Instead, they will be known for their adaptability to the many different challenges they face.

Personal brand and perception are critical for any leader, whether they are an aspiring or an experienced leader. Building your brand can have numerous benefits, some of which are:

Increases influence: A leader's personal brand and perception can increase their influence within the organisation and beyond. When a leader has a strong personal brand and a positive perception, it can increase their ability to influence others to achieve organisational goals.

Builds trust: A leader's personal brand and perception can build trust among employees, customers, and stakeholders. When a leader has a strong personal brand, it creates a sense of credibility and reliability, which can lead to increased trust.

Attracts talent: A leader's personal brand and perception can attract high performing individuals to the organisation. When a leader has a strong personal brand and a positive perception, it can make the organisation an attractive place to work.

Creates a highly engaged culture: A leader's personal brand and perception can influence the workplace culture. When a leader has a positive personal brand and perception, it can encourage employees to adopt similar behaviours, creating a positive workplace culture.

Enhances the reputation of the organisation: A leader's personal brand and perception can enhance the organisation's reputation. A leader with a positive personal brand and perception can help to build the organisation's reputation as a reputable and trustworthy entity.

In conclusion, a leader's personal brand and perception play a critical role in the success of an organisation. A leader with a strong personal brand and a positive perception can build trust, create a positive workplace culture, attract high-performing individuals, enhance the organisation's reputation, and increase their influence. Therefore, it is essential for leaders to invest in building their personal brand and perception to achieve these benefits.

Planning and time management

The second component of stage 4 is to give aspiring leaders an understanding of the criticality of time management and effective planning. Demands on leaders are ever increasing, yet we expect our leaders to be able to perform to a high standard, develop their teams, and meet the organisation's goals without any direction or support. We often set them up to fail. This module focuses on providing them with effective tools and techniques to better manage their time and plan effectively, such as Week in the Life of (WILO); prioritisation of tasks and initiatives; tips on effective emails management; and pointers on how to delegate.

WILO: A WILO is a simple tool that enables a leader to manage their diary more effectively. Key routines are scheduled into the leader's diary each week and time is allocated for activities such as (but not limited to):

- strategy time
- personal development
- *look, listen & learn* walks
- team one-to-ones
- team routines or meetings
- administration
- email and other communication channel management
- stakeholder management.

The idea is that you are achieving 80% + of your WILO adherence each week. Each time an allocated routine or slot is missed, the leader records the reasons on a separate chart. Over time, a trend may appear which will assist the leader to identify improvement opportunities. Having an effective WILO improves both a leader's capacity and their ability to focus on the activities that add the most value to the team and the organisation.

Prioritisation of tasks and initiatives: Fundamental to being an effective leader is an ability to prioritise their workload to ensure that they are focusing on the things that drive the most value for the organisation. We often see leaders on the dancefloor, firefighting, and spinning plates. This is often the sign of a leader who has not prioritised their workload effectively. Providing them with tools such as prioritisation matrices or PICK matrices and the knowledge to use the tools effectively will greatly assist the leader to focus on the initiatives and or tasks that are fulfilling the strategic direction of the company. The acronym PICK stands for the four possibilities: Possible, Implement, Challenge, and Kill. This is a visual tool for organising ideas and making decisions.

Effective email/other communication channel management and delegation: Email/other communication channel management is one of the biggest capacity drains on a leader's week. We often hear of leaders who spend upwards of 30% of their week bogged down in emails. Providing them with simple tools—such as the widely publicised 4 Ds (see below)—will improve their capacity to spend more time with their teams. Reallocating time from areas that add no real value to either the customer or their teams into areas such as time in field will create constancy of purpose. Leaders will be with their teams more and help them to connect what they do each day with the overall purpose of the organisation. In doing so, they start to create a foundation for a strong, sustainable, high-performing culture.

Delete it: Deleting emails is by far the quickest and easiest, method to create capacity and that's why it's first. When you first dive into your email management time block, go through your inbox and delete everything that is unimportant. Unsubscribe or block as many junk

153

emails as you can so you don't have to keep dealing with them every week. Setting up rules to automatically move certain emails or senders into a 'junk' file will minimise the distraction.

Do it: Once you have set up your rules and or deleted the non-important emails or junk out of your way, turn your attention to the emails that take relatively no time to close out. Generally, these are quick responses, with less than five minutes to action.

Delegate it: Not all emails need to be actioned by yourself. Often, it's good for a leader to delegate tasks to their teams to give them the ability to learn and grow. Ask, 'Could someone else in my team do this action?' If the answer is yes, then delegate to them and provide them the authority and power to do the task.

Defer it: Once you have done all of the above tasks, you should then be left with the more complex emails or actions. These are ones that generally will take longer to complete. These can be placed in a 'to do' folder or 'flagged' for follow-up later.

Stage 5—Managing performance and coaching systems

Stage 5 focuses on providing the up-and-coming leaders with the tools and knowledge to be able to coach their teams more effectively. We will discuss this further in Chapter 9.

This stage also focuses on the key component of managing poor behaviours and or repeated underperformance. We often see leaders pushing poor-performing colleagues or poor behaviours onto other leaders in other areas to deal with, while not dealing with the problem in the first place. Having a colleague who is not meeting the ideal behaviours or values of the organisation needs to be managed effectively, either by understanding the drivers for that underperformance or poor behaviour and helping them get back on track with an effective coaching plan or managing them out of the organisation. Not doing either of these two actions will start to diminish the culture you have created. A leader who doesn't manage this one person effectively can have a profound effect on everyone else.

> A leader who doesn't manage this one person effectively can have a profound effect on everyone else.

Stage 6—Resilience

In any leadership position, there will inevitably be challenges and obstacles that arise, and having a leader who is resilient and better equipped to deal with the difficulties that arise will ultimately deliver better outcomes for the organisation. This is an important skill for any leader to learn, for several reasons:

Perseverance: Resilient leaders can persevere through the many challenges that any situation can throw at an organisation. They can maintain a positive attitude, which then helps to motivate their teams during challenging times.

Adaptability: Resilient leaders can pivot and adapt to changing circumstances. They can quickly shift their strategies accordingly, which is an essential skill in today's world of VUCA.

Creativity: Resilient leaders are often great at problem-solving. They tend to look at different options to address new challenges. They often think creatively to find solutions in their ever-changing world.

Lead by example: Resilient leaders set an example for their teams and those around them, showing them how to overcome obstacles and challenges. They maintain a positive attitude in the face of adversity.

In summary, resilient leaders are better able to navigate the challenges that get thrown at them. They do so with positivity, which further lifts their teams to do the same.

Mental fitness and wellbeing:

Stage 6 focuses on the importance of being mentally fit and ensuring that your wellbeing is protected. Developing leaders who work on themselves first ensures that they are fit and strong to assist with others.

> Developing leaders who work on themselves first ensures that they are fit and strong to assist with others.

This component is of the utmost importance, and it focuses on all the tools and techniques that the organisation has at its disposal for its people. It helps individuals and leaders to connect back to the core belief system and assist them to better manage their emotions under duress or stressful situations. Leaders need to have mental fitness to be able to make sound decisions, manage their emotions effectively, and effectively communicate with their teams. A leadership role can be stressful, so having a leader who is able to deal with these stresses and pressures head on are more resilient when they face those setbacks or challenges.

Mental fitness also helps leaders to think more strategically and more creatively, which are essential competencies of any great leader. It enables them to perform at their best, make better decisions, and create a positive working environment for their teams. Leaders will often be wearing the adaptive leader hats of support, inspire, and coach in this context.

CASE STUDY FROM AN ASPIRING LEADER— JAMES OLSEN

In 2018, I made the decision to switch companies and start a new career in finance within the contact centre. In a short time, I could immediately see a difference in the leadership style throughout the area I worked in. There was a real drive for colleague development and engagement. It was clear to me that helping others grow and succeed was something I would gladly jump out of bed for in the morning and from that point on it was my driving force to become a leader.

The aspiring leader's program was announced shortly after my leadership development had started. This program was a first of its kind at our company and immediately captured my interest, as it appeared to provide a clear stepping stone into leadership. My leader at the time helped me draft up an expression of interest and, before I knew it, I was in the program.

This program was presented in stages and broke down the many foundations and principles of leadership, while still aligning them to real-life examples within the business and was often delivered in practical forms like roleplaying.

We had guest speakers throughout the program. One such speaker was I. Something that has always stuck with me was the vulnerability that he showed when he talked about his leadership journey. He relayed the message that it's okay not to be okay and to lean on those around you for support. As the saying goes, 'You can't pour from an empty cup.'

One of the program's highlights was its practical approach, offering us opportunities to step into leadership roles temporarily. This hands-on experience proved invaluable and shaped my understanding of leadership dynamics. Equally invaluable was the camaraderie among fellow aspiring leaders, a network of support that still endures, even four years after the program concluded.

Graduating from the program marked the beginning of my leadership journey. A six-month secondment provided the canvas for me to apply my newfound knowledge. Although I was eager to make an impact, I initially encountered challenges due to my haste to make a difference within the team. I learned a vital lesson: trust is the bedrock upon which leadership stands.

Guided by my mentor from the program, I successfully navigated these challenges. I believe it's important to state I did not get it right at first; however, I truly believe the support and guidance I received at this stage helped to shape the leader I am today. I always try to lead with vulnerability and humility and build a foundation of trust with those I work.

The aspiring leaders program helped me to start my career as a leader and, as such, I feel a profound urge to pay it forward. Several years into my leadership journey, I was honoured to facilitate the same program that had sculpted my leadership path. This experience allowed me to not only deliver the content but also share my firsthand experiences and how I grew as a new leader. Collaboratively, we worked to refine the program, aligning it with the esteemed Shingo Principles and enhancing its depth and relevance.

In retrospect, I believe that the aspiring leaders program delineated a clear pathway for emerging leaders. Its success story is echoed through the multitude of leaders it has nurtured. I firmly advocate that program.

In summary, the fundamental role of a good leader is to truly understand the potential of each of their team members. They need to take time to understand each individual at a deeper level, understanding what their centre of control is, what they value, and what their fundamental beliefs are. What are the things that make them 'tingle' at work? What is their underlying purpose? When a leader identifies this and then takes time to connect them to the overall organisational purpose, you will start to see levels of performance you could only dream of.

3 KEY TAKEAWAYS FROM THIS CHAPTER

1. Take time to understand each team member's purpose. Their *why* they come to work each day.

2. Use the different leadership hats to help team members connect their purpose to the organisations purpose.

3. See the true potential in every team member and create strong development pathways or systems to enable them to reach their full potential.

ACTIVITY 6

TABLE 6.1: Activity 6

ACTION	IDEAL BEHAVIOUR	ADAPTIVE LEADER HAT(S)
Identify 3 individuals that you will meet to understand their core belief system. 1. What motivates them? 2. What is their purpose? 3. Where do they want to be in 3 years' time?	Leader listens to understand the individual and takes action to define a set of actions to assist the person to achieve their true potential.	Inspire Teach Support Coach
Define your own purpose by writing down the top 10 things that make you 'tingle' at work. What are the moments that internally, make you fist pump the air with excitement?	Leader is engaged, passionate and inspiring those around them.	Inspire
Using the Talent Matrix as discussed in this chapter, (see fig 6.1) with your leadership team, map your direct reports and identify 3 key development actions for each one to assist them to reach their potential.	Leaders are seen to create strong development pathways for their teams.	Inspire Teach Support Coach

7

ORGANISATIONAL PURPOSE
Rowing the boat together

Working in an organisation that has a clear purpose which is communicated effectively through every layer ensures that every individual knows how they each contribute to the overall strategic direction of the company. Sounds easy right? Far from it.

This is probably the most difficult task for executive teams in any organisation. To deliver sustainable results that continue to improve year after year, senior leadership teams need to create systems that ensure every person in the organisation, at all levels, truly understands the direction and strategic goals of the company. They need to know the true north of where the company is headed and why the company exists. Wearing the Inspire hat is critical to supporting this.

Connecting every individual in the organisation to why the company exists creates a sense of belonging. People like to feel connected to something they believe in. The concept of a company's purpose has gained significant attention and importance in recent years, particularly when it comes to social responsibility and ethical considerations. A company's purpose goes beyond the traditional profit generation and focuses on the broader impact and contribution of the organisation to society and the environment.

> Creating a high-performing team requires every individual to be rowing the boat in the same direction.

The company's purpose defines why it exists, its core values, and the positive impact it can have on the community and future generations to come. The purpose of the organisation can have a profound impact on business performance, staff engagement, the communities in which it operates, and social responsibilities. In this chapter, we will focus on the first two: business performance and staff engagement.

Creating a high-performing team requires every individual to be rowing the boat in the same direction. If you have a leadership team where one or two leaders are rowing in a different direction, chaos will occur, and your business objectives may not be achieved. The team will become dysfunctional, often with poor behaviours evident. A clear and meaningful purpose can drive strong business outcomes in several ways:

- **Long-term vision.** An organisation whose purpose drives a long-term vision far beyond short-term goals and objectives. It helps you navigate the ever-changing world and challenges, which enables you to adapt to the market and environmental changes.
- **Competitive advantage.** A strong, purpose-driven company can differentiate itself from its competitors by aligning with its target markets. Customers are increasingly drawn to companies that prioritise environmental and social impacts.
- **Strategic focus.** A purpose is the north star that guides the decision-making of the organisation and provides a framework for setting the organisation's strategic goals. It helps the organisation to select and or prioritise initiatives that are aligned with the true north. Value Driver Tree is a tool that can assist leaders to select and prioritise tactical initiatives that will drive the strategic outcomes of the organisation.

VALUE DRIVER TREE

The purpose of a value driver tree (VDT), based on a concept first developed by DuPont, is to draw out the relationship between the elements that create value for an enterprise. It is intended to map out each element that feeds into a specific output and can be applied to visualise anything that will drive the desired output of the enterprise strategy, be it production output, new product development, zero injuries, etc.

The VDT is a map that shows all the ingredients at multiple levels that feed into any one of these macro outputs and are built separately for each focus area. By defining all elements, an organisation can then effectively pinpoint those that currently have the largest negative impact on delivering the desired value.

Key benefits can be seen as:

- A clear visualisation of how specific elements or metrics feed into the overall value creation.
- A way to identify key areas to focus on at various levels of the organisation to meaningfully impact the macro results.
- Providing a framework by which teams can think more deeply about impacts on results rather than those that are assumed to be obvious or today's news, ensuring that the root cause is not overlooked.
- While tracking progress as you move towards stable and sustainable delivery on these outputs becomes easier, so does setting improvement targets to move passed current plans.

Once defined, a VDT can then be created manually either on a whiteboard or through available software to provide an interactive view of the current state. The benefit of building in software is that you can test the accuracy of the VDT by creating different scenarios. For example, by changing an output to a target, you can see the impact at higher levels in the map: If we shift *availability* from 80% to 85%, what can we reasonably expect overall production outputs to move to?

HOW DO YOU BUILD A VDT?

The process is reasonably simple and can be done with nothing more than a whiteboard and a set of sticky notes and/or pens (see Figure 7.1 below). It is useful to gather all the key stakeholders together.

- Select the value driver that you wish to detail out (we may define this as A in Figure 7.1 below).
- Then brainstorm what are all the elements that directly feed into this output. As in the example below, we can see that B and C are the direct feeds in and that B + C = A.
- Continue this approach, following each branch in turn until you have exhausted the inputs. Below, we can see that B is achieved through the combination of D + E + F and that D is built up by G +H + J + K.
- Once we have exhausted the B branch, we do the same for C.
- Once both are built out, then review the whole tree level by level. Here we can see D+E+F+L+M = B+C.
- We then do a final brainstorm to check whether we have missed anything else and, if so, find where these elements fit into the whole VDT.

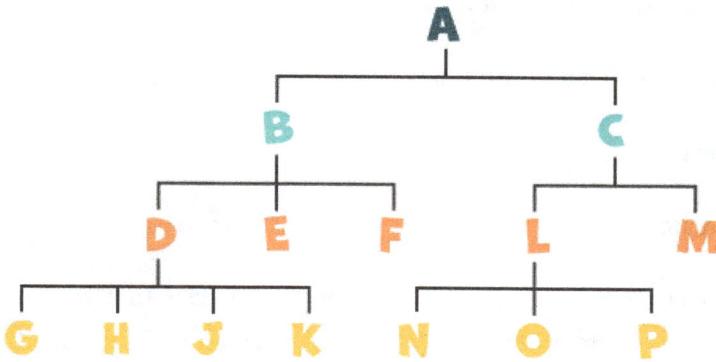

Figure 7.1: Example of a simple VDT design.

'SIMPLIFIED HOSHIN CASCADE'— TRUE NORTH THROUGH VALUE DRIVER TREE

In its simplest form, Hoshin Kanri principles are intended to drive shared decision making, resulting in a built consensus of the vital few things we must focus on. The process involves deploying a pre-existing strategy (there are many and varied frameworks in which you will build a coherent strategy), though it is only through deployment (roll out) and execution (implementation) that a strategy delivers real competitive advantage—the focus being on delivering effective and efficient (or excellent and sustainable).

How does a leader do it?

1. Define the organisational purpose.

2. Create a plan with analysis of both external and internal factors.

3. Devise the key strategic objectives.

4. Create your value driver tree.

5. Select from your value driver tree the metrics that are your key performance indicators (these will currently have the biggest impact on delivering the strategic objectives).

6. Cascade these metrics level by level through the business (from general manager to manager, manager to team leader to the front line).

7. Conduct a conversation at each level of the organisation (known as a catch-ball process) to evaluate its validity and how, in current circumstances, the key performance indicator (KPI) will drive appropriate behaviours to deliver the expected success levels. The catch-ball process may be a negotiation to find consensus.

Firstly, a catch-ball process involves gaining buy-in from the frontline, by setting the objective/requirement, asking them to work out what is required to deliver the objective, and inviting them to make any counteroffers they feel are necessary based on current status and gap closing responses. For example, if you ask a person to raise output of production by 100 tonnes a day they may counter with a request for one additional truck. Now, you may come back and both agree the target can be 50 tonnes per day by finding efficiencies.

Secondly, catch-ball horizontally is to agree the split of requirement at say manager level to feed onto management key performance metrics. For example, if production say they can run only 2% quicker, they may ask maintenance to increase availability by 5% to arrive at the same improved output.

It's essentially a negotiation to find consensus amongst your value stream both up and down the organisation.

8. Conduct the catch-ball step at each level to ensure horizontal alignment once the vertical cascade and escalation are agreed.

9. Deploy the KPI set once the vertical cascade and escalation are agreed.

10. Review the KPIs current performance versus target on a daily or weekly basis, as is appropriate for the level of work.

11. Review the plan periodically to ensure it remains contemporary. Finally, at appropriate touch points, review the planning system that enabled you to devise the plan.

12. Once you've determined your KPIs, it's a good opportunity to get each team to think about what ideal behaviours are needed to deliver the KPIs and what are some potential Key Behaviour Indictors (KBIs) they could measure. We will explore KBIs in more detail in chapter 10.

USING VDT TO DRIVE A HOSHIN PROCESS

The cascade is built up in a simple manner such as on a whiteboard, drawing out the process first then overlaying the Value Driver Tree. As each metric is understood, a decision is made whether this is a KPI or not (a KPI will be the vital few things that have the greatest impact on the organisation's success).

There may, of course, be many metrics that will continue to be measured and reviewed throughout the organisation. These are not ignored but will continue to be monitored until they adopt a critical impact to the broader business targets, at which point they may be promoted to a KPI.

As each metric is adopted as a KPI, we ensure clarity on the *what* and the *why* and this is then cascaded to the next level for the relevant owners to define the *how*.

HOSHIN AND KPI CASCADE PRINCIPLES

- Shared decision making resulting in consensus.
- Any KPI under a discreet macro metric at any level in the organisation will have an unbroken path to any other KPI in that organisation.
- Plans are created following real research into customer needs.
- Limited number deployed level by level in a participative manner.
- Each higher level offers the what and why while the next level down proposes the how.
- Work (with improvement activity) is conducted that directly reflects the KPIs and these are regularly reviewed and modified.
- When expected outcomes are not achieved it is the plan and planning process are challenged and examined, not the people.
- It is an ongoing process of learning to understand the system and its environment better (not a command and control approach).

CHANGE & COMMUNICATIONS SYSTEMS

Getting vertical alignment throughout your organisation is not an easy task. It requires strong leadership standard work systems to be in place as well as very effective change and communications systems to be evident to enable your frontline teams to connect to the overall purpose of the organisation. People absorb change in many ways. The one thing about any organisation is that change is constant and in the world of VUCA, this becomes a challenge for many leaders to lead their teams through.

We have worked with many organisations over the years and the majority we have come across don't necessarily understand the impact of not having an effective change and communications system in place. Some organisations do not invest in the management of change and rely solely on their leadership teams to design, rollout, and embed the changes they need in the organisation. They forget that change comes in many ways, for example:

External change factors:

- regulatory change
- customer trends changing
- environmental change
- economic and market change
- fiscal changes.

Internal change factors:

- training and development
- policy and procedural change
- technology changes
- product changes
- structural changes
- strategic direction changes
- company vision changes
- company values changing
- company-wide events (town halls, diversity and inclusion events, awards nights)
- people activities (performance reviews, employee surveys).

The above are only some of the external and internal changes that can impact a business's capacity to meet customer demand, as these changes require every individual in the company to be able to absorb the change, understand the change, and adapt to the change.

Failure to understand this very important component of your overall organisational systems will inevitably lead to increasing your risk of change not being understood on the front line. It leads to increased errors, defects, and reworks which, in turn, increases your costs.

> With change comes the potential to either increase or decrease the level of risk we are exposed to.

With change comes the potential to either increase or decrease the level of risk we are exposed to, referred to as **risk exposure**. Where we have seen organisations do this well is when they have a centralised change and communications function that designs, coordinates, and controls the flow of change to the front line. They have strong management-of-change systems in place that are closely monitored and controlled so the front line is not overloaded with change..

MANAGEMENT OF CHANGE SYSTEMS

One organisation we worked with controlled every bit of change that was designed. They created a management-of-change system (MoC) that had strict controls in place so that no change, no matter how big or small, could be delivered without going through this system for oversight, planning, and approval. They ranked each change in collaboration with the change initiators in order of impact on the front line. They rated their changes:

1. insignificant
2. low
3. medium
4. high.

The MoC tool encompassed three key assessments to help the leaders understand the size and impacts of the change:

1. The balancing capacity and demand impact assessment was a very early assessment of the impact of the change on the front line, customers, and the overall organisation
2. The balancing capacity and demand impact assessment asked certain questions that helped with the materiality of the change and how it would impact the business and the front line. These questions then drove an outcome that gave the ratings as detailed above. If the rating arrived at a medium or high impact, then the process moved to the third stage.
3. Detailed risk assessment involves a detailed assessment of the change and its impacts on the overall organisational risk profile and its people. This generally required a greater level of scrutiny by the senior leadership teams to ensure that the change being delivered did not impact any key controls or compensatory controls.

Most importantly, however, was that each of the changes, regardless of the rating, had to be entered into an organisation-wide change calendar. This calendar was a one-stop shop for the front line and leaders across the organisation to view change, communications, events, and people activities. This view enabled the smoothing out of change so that it minimised impacts on the front line and the ability of leaders to absorb the change. If one month was change heavy, the change team would work with the change initiators to level load the flow of change so that they re-risked the change absorption rates.

This system enabled **constancy of purpose**, which is another Shingo principle that ensures the golden thread of strategy deployment and information runs through the fabric of your organisation. This enables everyone to row the boat the same way. Communication is clear from the top down and it ensures that every individual knows what they need to do.

> Leaders fail to recognise the importance of understanding how the front line connects what they do to why they do it.

Sometimes, however, even with these strong systems in place, organisations fail to connect their teams on the front line to the overall purpose of the organisation. Leaders fail to recognise the importance of understanding how the front line connects what they do to why they do it.

To help with that understanding, we like to wear our coach hat, and coach leaders and teams in workshops to build their team customer value proposition (CVP). A CVP is, essentially, what customers are pulling from you. It's what the customer values from you.

FINDING TRUE NORTH
(Inspire Hat)

Recently, while I was coaching some senior leaders in the mining industry on the rollout of their purpose, they came to me for help as they couldn't understand why their teams were not connected to the organisational purpose.

The explanation I gave to the leaders was simply that advertising your purpose across the organisation and buying the teams gifts with 'Purpose' written on it will not lead to the teams intrinsically linking to the true north in what they do every day.

Leaders need to help them connect to the true north. This comes in two forms:

1. Build what they do every day to the organisations purpose.
2. Leadership shadow.

Build what they do every day to the organisational purpose:

This is where the leaders need to use a combination of three hats: coach, teach, and inspire. Linking what the teams do, day in and day out, to the organisational purpose is critical to the success of the team and the business. Leaders need to understand the context of each individual and proactively apply the hats as required to help their connection to the purpose. One of the best ways to achieve this vital connection is to collaborate with the team to devise their own CVP.

CASE STUDY

(Inspire Hat)

I coached a leader in the mining industry recently on this. His team was a maintenance function and struggled to connect to the overall organisational purpose.

I spent a couple of hours with the team. In the first part of the session, the maintenance crew defined who the team's customers were. Customers were defined as both upstream and downstream teams who relied on them to perform activities that created value for them. This helped the team to establish a clear understanding of their value stream and what was required of them to ensure that they provided value for them. The team came up with a CVP of 'Providing a safe, reliable service without compromising on quality'.

For a mining maintenance team, this was a fantastic CVP, as it was clear to the team that there were three key measures of success.

A good CVP will have two to three key measures within the statement. These measures are clear for the team so they know on any given day how they are tracking their CVP and creating value for their customers.

Safety was measured by the number of hazards identified and the number of injuries that occurred each week. Identifying hazards was key to ensuring the team continually improved and identified hazards before incidents occurred. The target for injuries was zero, so having a clear view of these each day helped the team to recognise areas for improvement.

Reliability was measured by the continuity of service of the plant that they oversaw. The better the work they performed, the lower the amount of plant downtime that occurred; therefore, the higher the production rates.

Quality was measured by the number of repeat breakdowns on the equipment they serviced or unplanned work. The lower the amount of unplanned work meant that their jobs were performed at a higher quality, which in turn then reduced waste in the system.

Having a clear CVP helps the team to know how they are performing each day against the overall business objectives and any deviations to performance are recorded. Repeat deviations are then problem-solved using practical problem-solving tools, such as Fishbone and 5 Whys.

I was doing a presentation to a team in the mining industry in 2022 on the connection of their new operating system to that of Shingo Principles. In the room was a broad range of team members. There were people from the production team, maintenance teams, and the services team.

When discussing the connection to purpose and their roles in achieving the organisation's strategic goals, one lady spoke out and said, 'But I am only the cleaner.' I immediately stopped the flow of the presentation and said to her, 'You're not *just* a cleaner. You helped put up to 20% of the world's electric vehicles on the road.'

She gave me a bemused look. I went on to explain that if she didn't perform her role to the best of her ability and keep the mine site clean and safe, they could be shut down for not meeting their health and safety standards. If that happened, the site couldn't meet its production targets and therefore they couldn't fulfil their customer's needs for a high-quality product.

Since then, the team she is a member of is one of the most engaged teams on site. Each morning at their pre-start routine, the cleaning team sings the purpose of the organisation collectively before going out to do their jobs to the best of their ability.

Adaptive Leadership Shadow:

To truly drive constancy of purpose throughout your organisation, you need each leader to continually speak to the purpose and vision of the business. Every time a leader writes a communication, they need to reference the organisation's vision and purpose. Every time they speak to a staff member, whether in their team or another team, they need to continually refer the work they are doing back to the overall vision or purpose of the organisation. This is where they wear the inspire hat. They connect their staff and what they do to the overall true north of the company.

> You need each leader to continually speak to the purpose and vision of the business.

CASE STUDY

(Support Hat)

When I used to lead a large contact centre, I built a daily repetitive rhythm into my leader standard work. The company used an external platform for collecting real-time voice of the customer feedback. Each day, I would receive hundreds of customer feedback surveys, rated 0–10. A score of 9 or 10 was a promoter; they would recommend the company to their family and friends. A score of 0–6 was a detractor. A detractor was a customer who was dissatisfied with the company and wouldn't recommend the organisation to their family and friends. A score of 7 or 8 was identified as a passive customer.

Every morning, I would review the previous day's customer feedback and select four or five promoters. Putting on my Support and Inspire hat, I would then email the staff member who had dealt with those customers to recognise them for an excellent job, while linking their behaviour back to the organisation's vision. This simple daily ritual had a significant impact on staff morale and focus on the customer experience.

This small, repetitive ritual helped the organisation to grow its net promoter score (NPS) by 315% over three years, which was an incredible result. It was a leadership shadow that was cast over all leaders in the business. Once I had done this every day for a period, the rest of the leadership group all started to do the same. The result was to lift the focus by team members on customer experience to a level we never expected when we started. It also helped to connect staff to the organisation's vision, which created a sense of pride across the business.

We also looked at the detractors each day and identified areas for improvement. These detractors were fed into their weekly continuous improvement routine. Both repetition of recognition and reinforcing the link between the employees' behaviours and the vision or purpose helped the organisation to achieve global best-in-class standards of excellence.

ENTERPRISE ALIGNMENT VALUE DELIVERY

We have spoken about vertical alignment and creating that connection to the true north of the organisation. This is critical to the organisation's success; however, equally; you need to have horizontal alignment to create true value or organisational alignment.

We often see an organisation's functions working in silos, where they individually deliver on their key performance indicators; however, this often ends up with short-term results.

Driving long-term, sustainable results requires a different mindset.

Driving long-term, sustainable results requires a different mindset. It requires each of your leaders and teams to work collaboratively and collectively across the value stream. We see this in new, agile operating models where there are multi-disciplined teams or squads working collectively on a defined customer outcome.

This sort of operating model creates value at pace. They remove the waterfall project management approaches, with their multi-layers of approvals and red tape, and replace it with an agile, pace-over-perfection mindset of delivery.

SILO VALUE DELIVERY

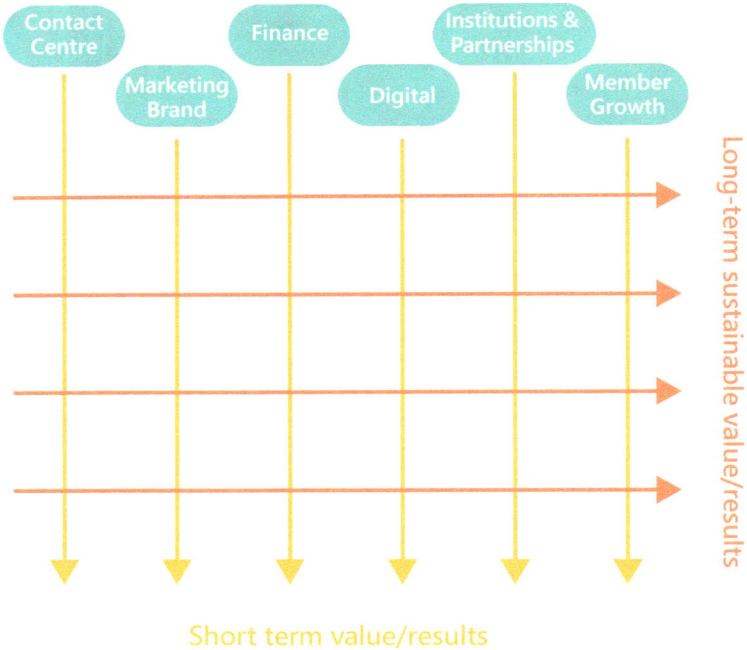

FIGURE 7.2: Enterprise alignment value delivery model

These operating models are challenging for organisations to implement; however, we can still achieve similar results when we think systemically. Thinking systemically is another enterprise alignment principle of Shingo. This principle teaches us to align our management systems, principles, and tools so that we can drive sustainable results. Everyone in the organisation has a deep understanding of the value stream and can understand the processes and systems in each area (Hines et al 1998). In doing so, you start to create systems that drive a reduction of waste throughout the value stream; you know what is required upstream to ensure the widget you are producing or the service you are providing flows through to the customer at minimal cost and interruption.

Having the vertical alignment and horizontal alignment working in unison will start to create a high-performing culture. That said, it will start to come under strain unless you underpin the culture with a strong reward and recognition system. People want to feel connected to a higher purpose; however, they also want to be recognised for their individual and collective contributions to the success of the organisation. Having a strong reward and recognition system will inevitably inspire a high-performing culture.

> Having the vertical alignment and horizontal alignment working in unison will start to create a high-performing culture.

A strong reward and recognition system will serve as a catalyst for employee motivation. When employees are recognised, they feel valued and appreciated. They come to work each day motivated to put in one hundred percent. They feel a profound sense of connection to the purpose and vision of the organisation. They become driven to achieve their goals and exceed expectations. By aligning rewards with desired outcomes, you can channel your employee's efforts toward organisational objectives, resulting in enhanced productivity and superior performance.

Reward and recognition systems can foster a collaborative and cooperative work environment. By recognising team achievements and promoting collaboration, the organisation reinforces the value of teamwork and encourages employees to work together towards shared goals. In doing so, the organisation will start to break down silos and teams will start to work collaboratively to drive enterprise alignment and long-term sustainable value or results.

Reward and recognition systems play a key role in shaping and reinforcing the desired culture within an organisation. By recognising ideal behaviours and achievements that align with the company's overall strategic direction and values, the organisation can foster a culture of enterprise excellence, continuous improvement, and continuous learning.

Having a strong culture then starts to get noticed in the market. The shallow talent pools that were there previously start to be no more. The organisation starts to become one that people want to join. You start to attract top talent whilst reducing your attrition rates. It fosters a sense of loyalty and job satisfaction.

As mentioned earlier, a simple recognition or thank you for doing a good job goes a long way to make your team feel connected and valued. Reinforcing this recognition repeatedly will foster a great sense of pride that will assist you to drive sustainable long-term results.

3 KEY TAKEAWAYS FROM THIS CHAPTER

1. To connect your people to the company's overall purpose requires leaders to be consistent in connecting their people to the company's overall purpose and vision. This requires reinforcement and repetition every day, everywhere, and with everybody.

2. Alignment from the company CEO through to the frontline operator requires strong leadership and communications systems.

3. Leaders need to work across the value stream and become enterprise leaders to drive better outcomes for the organisation.

Table 7.1: Activity 7

ACTION	IDEAL BEHAVIOUR	ADAPTIVE LEADER HAT(S)
Identify 5-6 front line colleagues that work in the same team. In a workshop format, ask them to articulate the following: 1. Who are their customers? 2. What is it that their customers want from them? 3. How do they know they are meeting their customers requirements and expectations? 4. What metrics do they currently have that drive the customer value? If they can't articulate who or what their customers value and they can't clearly articulate what metrics they have in place to drive value, then their Hoshin alignment is not correct and further action is required to build a clear CVP and Hoshin metrics.	Leaders are seeking to connect the work their teams do to the overall organisation's strategy. They are ensuring that the teams are working on the right activities that drive value to the customer.	Inspire Teach Coach
Seek out customer feedback on your team's interactions and/or service they have provided in the last month. Create a weekly or monthly communications plan to recognise individuals who have delivered exceptional customer service or value to the customer. Recognise them for their efforts and link their actions to the overall purpose or vision of the organisation. Build a consistent and repetitive routine to do this on an ongoing basis.		Inspire Support

8

ENSURE THE FLOWER IS BLOOMING

You often hear sayings that ring true in so many ways such as this one widely attributed to Alexander Den Heijer:

> When a flower doesn't bloom you fix the environment in which it grows, not the flower.

This quote sums up what leadership excellence is and the intent of creating a culture that is centred around your people. To be an effective leader, you need to be selfless and one hundred percent committed to identifying the true potential of every individual in your team. Whether they are your most senior staff or the cleaner who comes in each day to maintain a safe and clean workplace, everyone is treated with the same level of respect. How you treat the one, influences the many.

Every individual has infinite capacity to grow in ability, so as a leader your people assets are critical to the success of your business and your future sustainability.

> Every individual has infinite capacity to grow in ability.

One of the most powerful principles that we discussed in chapter 4 is **respect for every individual**. The intent of this principle goes beyond the mere treating everyone with the same level of respect; it goes to the core of enterprise excellence. It's about looking deeper into every individual's beliefs, values, and behaviours. It's about looking at every individual, deep into the core of their existence: why they come to work each day, what drives them, what is their core purpose in life, and what is their true potential.

Seeing people's true potential and creating a strong development plan to help them achieve their true potential unlocks a level of performance and engagement that they could only dream of having. If you do this for every individual across your organisation, you will achieve results that are ideal. Ideal results are sustainable and desired by any leader.

For nearly three decades, I have led teams from many different functions and businesses, both in Europe and Australia. I have studied the methods for creating a high-performing, sustainable culture.

The word 'sustainable' is important to understand. While you can achieve results by driving a culture of delivery of outcomes, these results and outcomes are then generally followed by steep declines in performance for various reasons. Driving a culture of delivery of outcomes can achieve spot results but at the cost of your people. There tends to be higher unplanned sick leave, staff attrition, and lower engagement. A culture that likes to firefight and is reactive in nature is created.

> Driving a culture of delivery of outcomes can achieve spot results but at the cost of your people.

Over many years, I developed a formula to create a high-performing culture that will sustain an organisation through the many challenges it faces. The formula I have ended up with has been assessed successfully over the years and has helped leaders drive a strong culture that drives outstanding results.

HIGH PERFORMANCE = (CHARACTER + BEHAVIOURS + VULNERABILITY) - INTERFERENCE

High Performance = (C + B + V) – I

Let's look at the formula in a bit more detail. An organisation's high performance (HP) requires individual character (C) plus ideal behaviours (B) plus individual vulnerability (V) minus people's interference (I). High Performance (HP) requires leaders to think longer term. They need to build systems that will develop their people to their true potential, which in turn will drive results that are sustainable. A high-performing culture will enable every individual across all levels to feel empowered to effect change. They will drive long-term, sustainable results for their customers, shareholders, and communities.

As mentioned earlier, you can still achieve performance outcomes even with poor behaviours or a bad culture; however, this is not sustainable and will never drive the organisation towards enterprise excellence. That culture relies heavily on a small number of individuals to drive the results. More often, these results are short-lived and achieve short-term goals, usually over one to three years.

HP = (Character + B + V) - I

Character speaks heavily to the second foundational, culture-enabling principle of Shingo: *lead with humility*. To be a person of high character, you must be humble. Humility and character are so closely linked that you can't have one without the other. As a leader, you need to self-reflect in the first instance. You need to look at your inner self and dig deep into the *why* that drives you. If you are there to drive results to self-proclaim and clamber over others to get what you want, then you may achieve results but you will not achieve sustainable results. You certainly won't gain the respect of your teams and they certainly won't follow you.

We all want good people on our teams. We want people of sound character. Good people who do good things in their personal lives are the ones who create perfect team members. We don't want a team of individuals. We want a team of people who will work collaboratively, speak up when something is not right, work collectively to solve problems, and support each other to be better tomorrow than they were today.

Leading with humility is thinking 'we' not 'I'. It goes beyond personal preferences and ideologies. Having leaders and teams who think of others before they think of themselves creates a strong culture that is hard to break.

Character defines every individual. Your character is what people remember you by. To be of strong character, you must be reliable, have high integrity, and be humble and honest. As a leader, you want people on your bus who you can trust and who have high integrity.

> To be of strong character, you must be reliable, have high integrity, and be humble and honest.

Trust and integrity can be earned. It takes time to build; however, if you truly understand and embed the two foundational, culture enabling principles that Shigeo Shingo teaches us—*lead with humility* and *respect every individual*—you'll quickly create a culture where every individual comes to work each day bringing their true authentic self. They feel safe to speak up and challenge the standards. They work harder and they are continuously looking to improve the way they work, for both themselves and your customers.

The quote mentioned in chapter 3 by Edgar Schein perfectly demonstrates the importance of leaders managing the culture, rather than allowing the culture to manage them:

> The only thing of real importance that leaders do is to create and manage culture. If you do not manage culture, it manages you, and you may not even be aware of the extent to which this is happening.

If you have people on your team who are not of sound character and you fail as a leader to identify and manage those poor behaviours, you will not create the culture you desire. Having people in your team who display subversive or passive-aggressive behaviours will destroy your culture over time. These individuals feed off your culture, taking a bite at a time, and will undermine everything you are trying to do. If not managed correctly, the people who do demonstrate the ideal behaviours will leave.

Some leaders managed to turn individuals around using their coach hat. They provided an unobstructed vision of what acceptable behaviours would be in the future. However, some colleague's values and purpose just did not align with the company's and therefore they had to wear the direct hat and make tough decisions to let them go.

HP = (C + Behaviours + V)—I

As mentioned previously, you can still achieve results with poor behaviours. I am sure you would at some time in your working life have come across a leader who has driven an outcome for the organisation in a way that was sub-optimal. They could have managed the outcome through fear, driving people to do the work to achieve the results. You often see this in command and control type organisations. They manage, they do not lead and there is a massive difference.

When you manage people, you may get the short-term outcomes you wish for; however, you will not get sustainable results. You will not create a strong, continuous improvement culture and you certainly will not win your people over, that is for sure.

Creating and managing culture takes time. We often build our strategy or business goals and then look at the systems we need to build to get us our results and wonder why we achieve results that are not sustainable or that we have pockets of poor behaviours dotted around the organisation, slowly eating away at the culture.

The first two of the first three Shingo insights mentioned in chapter 3 guide us to creating a strong culture that would withstand the many challenges that organisations face: (1) Ideal results require ideal behaviours; and (2) Purpose and systems drive behaviours. We should look at the strategic objectives or business goals (the outcomes we want to achieve), then ask ourselves the question: What are the ideal behaviours we need to see and, as leaders, demonstrate across the organisation that will get us to our objectives? Once we define these, it's then and only then do we design the systems and or processes that we need that drive those agreed behaviours.

If you look at Figure 8.1 below, *The ideal behavioural change matrix,* you can clearly see that while management-driven behaviours will initially achieve results, these will disappear over time. It's like the shooting gun analogy. You fire the gun; the bullet rises at speed for a period before losing velocity and trajectory. On the other hand, when you build and embed ideal behaviours across every level of the organisation, while the results take longer to come to fruition, they are ones you have only ever before dreamt of achieving. Your people feel empowered and come to work each day as their true authentic

You create a continuous improvement culture of everybody identifying and improving, everywhere, every day.

selves, looking to improve their lives and the lives of their customers. You create a continuous improvement culture of everybody identifying and improving, everywhere, every day.

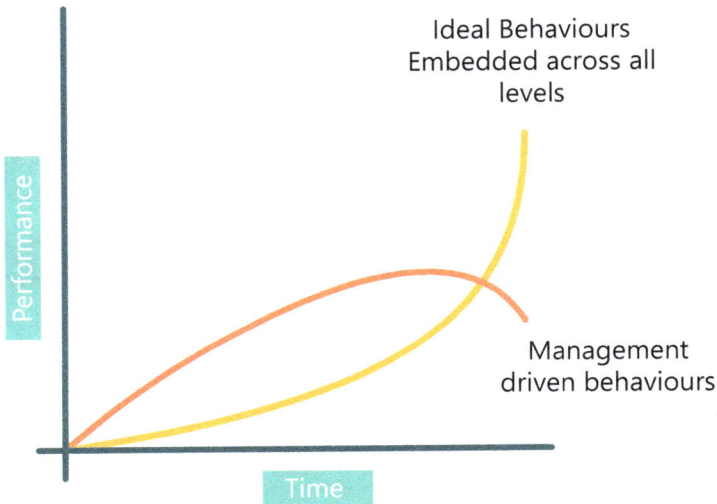

FIGURE 8.1: Ideal behavioural change matrix.

HP = (C + B + Vulnerability) - I

When you speak of vulnerability too often, we immediately jump to the thought of weakness and opening oneself up to potential harm. This can also be true of leadership in a command-and-control environment.

The essence of leadership vulnerability is what drives people to connect with you. You are seen as being human. It takes great courage for a leader to show vulnerability. Again, linking back to *leading with humility* that we spoke of earlier in the chapter, leaders don't have all the answers and that's okay. You are not expected to; however, what you are expected to know is how to connect with your people who, collectively, will have all the answers. They are the people who are closest to your customer.

They are the people who are working in the systems that the executives and managers have created, so they are the people who can tell you how to improve them.

People don't want robots as leaders, they want authenticity. They want leaders who are not afraid to say they got it wrong or that they have made mistakes. They want leaders to be vulnerable and show their true authentic selves. When leaders do this, they win the hearts and minds of their people. When you win the hearts and minds of your people, you create an environment of trust, respect, and continuous improvement.

> It takes great courage for a leader to show vulnerability.

CASE STUDY

(Support Hat)

A few years ago, I was promoted to a general manager (GM) position. This was something I had always aspired to; however, it was one that taught me one of the biggest lessons in my life.

As a new GM, you feel that you must hide your kinks, that you can't show your true self for fear of showing weakness in your armoury. At least, that's what I thought initially when getting the role. As I was progressing up the career ladder, an old work colleague used to always say to me, 'As you move up the organisational food chain, the lonelier it gets.'

I never really thought about it too much, until I got the role as GM. It's not lonelier if you have the courage to show vulnerability. However, I didn't see that at first. I was more concerned with ensuring that I put on a game face every day, that I was invincible, and that I could manage anything that came my way. How wrong was I.

As with the earlier quotation from Edgar Schein with regard to managing culture, the same principle can apply to mental wellbeing: 'The only thing of real importance that leaders do is manage wellbeing. If you do not manage wellbeing, it manages you, and you may not even be aware of the extent to which this is happening.'

This was so evident in my own case. I was plodding along in the new GM role, not aware that I was slowly eating away at myself. I was slowly entering a spiral that before I knew it, I was spinning out of control. I didn't see any warning signs. I wasn't aware that it was happening to me, and I certainly wasn't aware of the extent to which it was happening.

The role was challenging enough in itself and my own insecurities and fear of showing vulnerability drove me into a spiral of self-doubt. I was coming home every evening and slumping on the couch. My wife and kids were speaking to me, but I wasn't listening. All I could hear were mumbles but nothing was registering.

I would fall asleep at the drop of a hat, sometimes in the middle of a conversation with my kids. I felt lethargic all the time. I would toss and turn at night, waking myself up at night to send emails to myself as my mind raced about what I needed to do, and what actions I needed to take the following day.

The alarm would sound at 5 a.m. for my daily gym session—something I loved to do each day—but now I struggled to get my head off the pillow. I would eventually talk myself around and drag myself out of bed and off to the gym. This was a spurt of energy that would slowly disintegrate as the day moved on. Like Groundhog Day, the routine became all too familiar. Months went by and I went further around that spiral of uncontrol.

It all came to a head one Sunday morning. A friend of mine had invited me to a corporate event at a nearby golf club. The drive to the club was along the coast road, where all I could see was the crashing waves. It looked surreal and inviting. I drove into the golf club car park, still with the vision of the waves deep in the back of my mind. I pulled up, turned off the ignition, and sat, weeping into my hands wanting it all to end. Those waves were pulling me. All I wanted to do was to drive in and not return. I had unknowingly fallen so far into that spiral that I didn't know how to pull myself out.

I managed to pluck up the courage and call my wife. She could hear the sheer panic my voice and immediately dropped what she was doing, and we talked. I talked, and she listened. It gave some minor relief. We agreed during the call that we would discuss a plan that evening when I got home from golf. She assured me all would be ok. For now, she insisted I put it behind me and try to enjoy the game of golf as best I could. That I did; I put it securely locked away for later.

That night we sat and talked for hours. She talked me off that perch. She helped me stop the spiral and they agreed on a firm action plan. That plan centred around me having the courage to be vulnerable and seek out someone to wear the support hat for me.

The next day, I went to work with a plan. I was going to be vulnerable and ask for help. At the weekly check-in routine, I had my chance. I delved deep and uttered the words, 'Team, I am drowning. I need help.' I went on to explain the situation in more detail as the room of GMs listened intently. Just speaking the words, lifted me into a place of acceptance. I felt human again.

I was surprised at the reaction I received. They all came to help. Three of us agreed to a follow-up meeting where we all brainstormed the issues and produced a plan. We agreed on a 'Trio', where the three of us would catch up each week to debrief on the week's events. We created a safe environment for the three of us to download our thoughts and concerns. The GM's helped pull me out of that downward spiral I was in. I am forever grateful to them.

That gave me one of the biggest lessons my life: 'Never take a job for money or title. Go to where you are most alive and tingling at work and what if you can replicate that many times over.'

I took this harsh lesson into my next role, where I wore my heart on my sleeve. I had no issues about showing that vulnerability and when I spoke of my previous scenario, it paved the way for many other leaders and colleagues who also felt the same way to speak up. They spoke about their situations openly, which helped to create a strong, safe-to-speak-up culture.

> This is when I added the 'V' to the formula. I coached leaders and aspiring leaders on how to be their true selves, to not have an alter ego or game face, and instead to be themselves, be vulnerable and win the hearts and minds of their people.

HP = (C + B + V) - Interference

Interference has the most impact on the formula for creating a high-performing culture. We spoke earlier about leaders needing to understand the context within which every individual is operating before reacting. Leaders need to pause, think, and respond.

As discussed in chapter 3, leaders need to be aware that every individual has some sort of interference in their lives. When we look at interference, it can come in many forms. Interference can be either intrinsic or extrinsic. Everyone's behaviour and/or performance is impacted by either intrinsic or extrinsic interference, yet historically we have been coaching leaders to people manage performance.

'Never blame people, blame process.'

The late W. Edward Deming stated: 'Never blame people, blame process.' His studies, conducted over a career of working in post-war manufacturing companies, found that only 5% of the defects that occurred in those organisations were due to people error; 95% were caused by an ineffective system or process.

People come to work each day to do a decent job. When they have an error, risk event, or cause a defect, 95% of the time it is because of an ineffective process or system. Yet we coach our leaders to manage their performance. We should be coaching our leaders to go to *Look, Listen and Learn* and understand why the error occurred in the first place. Was it because our standard operating procedure wasn't clear enough? Was it that we never provided the right training? Did management create a pressurised environment in which to work? I could go on. How often have you met a stakeholder whose behaviour during that meeting was out of character, from left field and left you somewhat bemused? Normally, our reaction is, 'Where did that come from?'

What the **vulnerable** part of the formula teaches us to do is to understand the interference. Once a leader invests time into understanding that interference, they can then *dance with the interference*. They can put their support hat on and put mechanisms in place to help that individual through their challenges. When they do, they unleash a level of performance out of the ordinary. The person feels heard and understood. They feel respected at work and give one hundred percent of their true authentic selves.

Let us look at them in isolation.

Intrinsic interference

Intrinsic interference can be anything that impacts the thoughts and feelings of a person. Some of these can be hereditary and some can be a combination of life events that have occurred over the years.

Intrinsic interference is like the negative monkey in your brain that erodes your confidence, state of mind, and self-belief. Intrinsic interference can be things like self-doubt, anxiety, depression, and ADHD, to name a few.

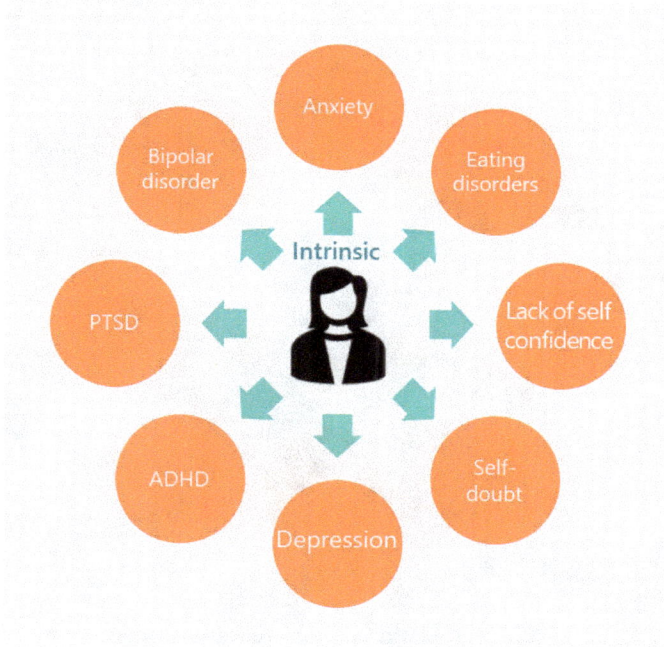

FIGURE 8.2: Intrinsic interference examples.

Extrinsic interference

Extrinsic interference is all the external factors that could impact a person's thoughts, feelings, or actions. These are impeding factors that can cause individuals to lower their ability to perform at an elevated level. Extrinsic interference can be things like top-down target pressures, workplace bullying, domestic abuse, financial abuse, drug and/or alcohol abuse, elder abuse, marital strains, teenager challenges, etc.

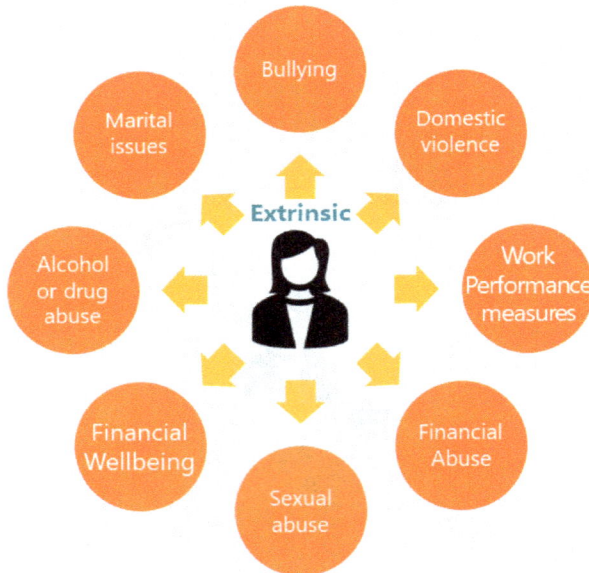

FIGURE 8.3: Extrinsic interference examples.

CASE STUDY

(Support Hat)

When I was previously leading a large team, they had one colleague—whom we'll call Jess—who was working in one of my support teams looking after one of our top customer segments. Jess was a high performer who continually met targets each month. She was a quiet achiever who came to work each day and put in a hundred per cent.

About a year into her tenure, her performance suddenly dropped off the page. She was in the lower performance bracket, which baffled the leadership team. Before coaching this formula to senior leaders, the usual course of action was to put on their direct hat, have a one-to-one discussion, and more than likely put her on a performance improvement coaching plan to try and bring her back in line with expectations.

On this occasion, however, her two-up leader put his support hat on and took the time to understand the interference that was impacting on Jess's performance. It took a few weeks to earn sufficient trust so that Jess could be her true self and open up to her two-up leader.

As it turned out, Jess was undergoing the lengthy and demanding process of transitioning to become Thomas. This was a massive change for Thomas as well as a massive challenge for myself and the leadership team, so we had to think of both his journey as well as the team's journey through this transition.

We immediately went into change and communications planning mode. We built a robust change and communications plan around how they would support the team and Thomas. It was a challenging time for the team also, as they dealt with issues such as which toilet Thomas would use, how to act around Thomas, what they could and couldn't say, and how they could show respect for his decision and support him on his journey. Coincidently, the organisation was implementing components of its diversity strategy and one of the initiatives was to have a non-binary toilet installed. This enabled Thomas to feel more comfortable, the leadership team gave him time off to have his hormone treatment and developed a strong change and communications plan to support his team through his transition.

Suddenly, Thomas's performance improved considerably. He went from strength to strength and exceeded all of his KPIs for that financial year.

The day I left the business; Thomas came to me in the kitchen area and thanked me for understanding his interference. He stated that he felt more support from the leadership team and within his own team than he did in his private life. To me, this tugged on an inner cord. I felt the organisation had positively impacted Thomas's life forever. We had understood his interference and danced with it.

3 KEY TAKEAWAYS FROM THIS CHAPTER

1. People's behaviours are always driven by something going on in their environment. It's the role of the leader to truly understand every individual's intrinsic and extrinsic interferences and dance with it.

2. If you want change to be sustainable, you must enable and empower your teams to lead the change.

3. Have the courage to be vulnerable. Those leaders who do connect more with their people.

ACTIVITY 8

TABLE 8.1: Activity 8.

ACTION	IDEAL BEHAVIOUR	ADAPTIVE LEADER HAT(S)
Identify 2 individuals in your team or organisation that have displayed one of the following characteristics in the last 3 months: 1: Underperformance 2: Erratic or poor behaviour Take the time to meet with them on an individual basis to seek to understand their intrinsic and/or extrinsic interference(s) and how that has impacted them. Note, it can take time to build trust so suggest you do this outside of the office environment – take them for a coffee etc. Once you understand their interference, work with them to put in place support mechanisms or systems that will help them.	Leader listens to understand the individual and defines a set of actions to assist the person progress to their true potential.	Inspire Teach Coach Support

9

LISTEN TO UNDERSTAND
Two ears, two eyes, one mouth

From our experience as leaders, it feels like there are always more things to do than time available. Just pause and ask yourself if this is true for you. Do you have a long list of things you need to get done? Are you constantly reorganising your priorities? Do you find yourself being the first person in the building and the last to leave?

For some of us, this feels acceptable because we are doing something we love; but even then, it may be stopping us from doing other important things. For others, it may be stopping us from enjoying life to the full or could even be causing issues with our personal relationships.

So, when someone comes along with the latest shiny new management theory and tells us we need to spend more time on the front line with our people, our natural reaction is to think, 'And when I am supposed to find time to do that?'

'What am I spending my time on?'

This is where it's useful to take some time out and reflect. Ask yourself: 'What am I spending my time on?'

You can categorise your time into three very broad groups:

- Day-to-day stuff e.g. dealing with problems, fixing issues, firefighting, etc.
- Working on continuous improvement: planned sustainable improvements rather than short-term firefighting, supporting teams to implement improvements.
- Working on the culture you want in the business: supporting people by managing and recognising great behaviours, supporting people, coaching people, inspiring people, teaching people, and, when needed, being directive.

Don't worry about being too exact about this. Just have a go - in a typical day or week, what does your time allocation looks like.

Figure 9.1 is an example from myself showing approximate hours spent each day:

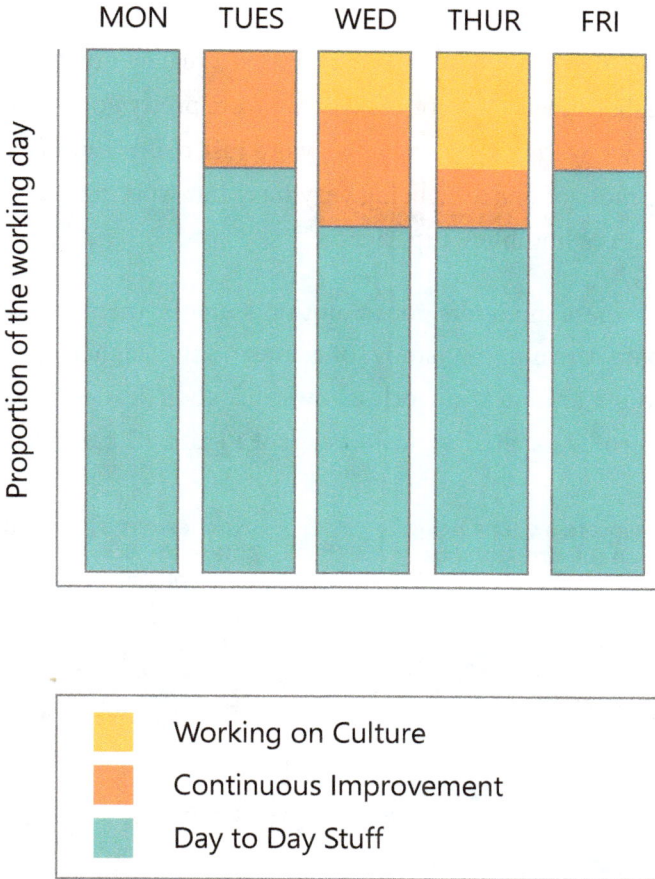

FIGURE 9.1: Example of how I spend my time being very busy working on the wrong things.

SO WHAT?

When we did this exercise ourselves, it was a real eye-opener for all of us. We realised that while we thought we were pretty good at managing our time, we weren't. In reality, we were just really good firefighters: spending most of our time being very busy but working on the wrong things. It was a humbling experience.

However, these numbers mean nothing unless there is something to compare them to. A study of some of the highest performing organisations around the world shows that their leaders have a very different profile for their typical week (see Figure 9.2 below).

How I allocate my time being busy on the wrong things

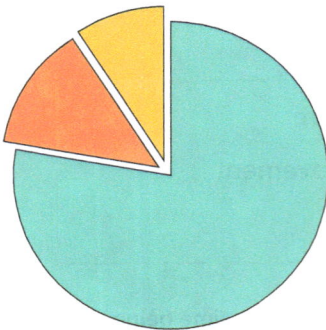

How leaders allocate their time in the best performing organisations.

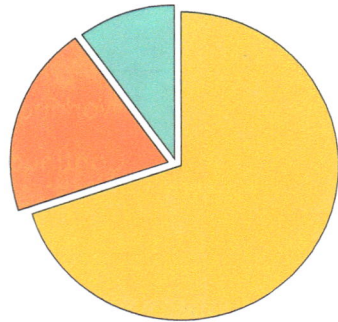

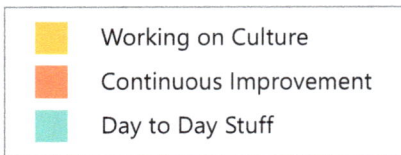

Working on Culture

Continuous Improvement

Day to Day Stuff

FIGURE 9.2: How leaders allocate their time in some of the best performing organisations in the world. Adapted from Hines and Butterworth 2019.

This might seem unrealistic and, to be fair, can be a bit daunting. However, once you start to review how you allocate your time and make deliberate choices, the profile can change very quickly. Here is a list of the typical things that could come under *working on culture*:

- Reinforcing the ideal behaviours (support hat).
- Correcting poor behaviour (direct hat).
- Recognition (support hat).
- Attending team huddles (support hat).
- Coaching (support hat).
- Training people in continuous improvement (teach hat)
- Working on diversity and inclusion (inspire hat).
- Working on people development (inspire hat).
- Working on personal development (inspire hat ref leading by example).
- One-on-ones with direct reports and 2-down (potentially all hats)
- Plan time for reflection (potentially all hats).
- Listen, Look, Learn activities (potentially all hats)

Most leaders are fairly good at putting together a plan to achieve a particular goal once the goal is clear. Once you know what good looked like, you can set a clear goal for getting better and put in place a Plan, Do, Check, Adjust (PDCA) plan to help you get there. Here's an example template. As we discussed in Chapter 1 you need triggers to help build new habits. Going through the PDCA cycle multiple times and reviewing actual v plan will help you to build new habits in how you consciously allocate your time.

Plan

Set goal for target time allocation to work on culture.

Decide what day-to-day stuff you will stop doing or delegate.

Plan out a fixed schedule for *Look, Listen, Learn* activities.

Review which meetings you attend and review the agenda for those you decide to continue to attend.

Do

Implement the plan.

Check

At the end of each week, do a quick review of your time allocation to see how you're doing.

Act/Adjust

If on plan, carry on. If not on plan, then review what needs to change and implement the changes for the following week.

Some people find it useful to track this on a visible chart but that's entirely up to you. If you find this useful, then great. If not, then just keep a note in your diary at the end of each week. Remember, we are not looking for precision to the hour here but aiming for a big shift in focus.

An Example Plan

Goal

Increase time allocated to working on culture to 30% in three months (need to free up 11 hours so I can allocate a total of 15 hours a week to working on culture).

WHAT WILL I STOP?

TABLE 9.1: What will I stop doing?

Activities I can stop	Hours per week freed up
Several meetings that I can delegate immediately.	4
Other meetings I can trust other people to lead with some coaching.	5
Taking on everyone else's problems and instead coaching them on how to solve them.	1
Not agree to do stuff without first working out the impact on how I want to spend my time.	1

WHAT WILL I DO INSTEAD?

TABLE 9.2: Time allocation plan to get to 30% time working on culture?

Activity	Hours per week
Allocate fixed time slots for Look, Listen, Learn activities.	4
Change the agendas of leadership meetings and allocate more time to working on the culture.	2
Attend huddle meetings.	2
Increase my one-on-one coaching sessions to twice monthly for all direct reports.	3
Start doing 2-down one-on-one coaching sessions.	1
Allocate weekly reflection and review time on how things are going with new time allocation.	1
Pause before giving people a solution and help them to work through it for themselves (build capability rather than dependence).	2

In reality, some actions are easier to quantify than others, but it was a good starting point and enables tracking of actual against a goal. In this example, after three months, the time allocated was being achieved and the impact on the culture was very positive.

The next plan was to get to 50% of time allocated to culture by the end of another six months. This challenge took nearer to 12 months but was worth it, with several tangible benefits such as:

- Employee engagement and retention figures dramatically improved.
- Meetings were much more positive and productive.

- People were fixing issues.
- Firefighting was reduced and we had more time to work on continuous improvement.
- All leaders had more time to work on the right things.
- Output and profits increased.

LOOK, LISTEN, LEARN

One of the most impactful things that helps shift the focus to working on culture is the implementation of structured Look, Listen, Learn (LLL) activities. These are most commonly referred to as *Gemba* walks but calling them out as *Look, Listen, Learn* activities helps remind us of the real purpose.

Unfortunately, in many organisations, these activities have become just something else that leaders have to do to 'tick a box' and they provide little real value. There seems to be a tendency to set targets for leaders to do X number of walks, without any real focus on the purpose or the quality of the activity.

> Let's be clear on the purpose before we jump into the activity.

The more successful organisations are training leaders on how to do an effective LLL activity. But, while it's important to understand this, the most critical place to start is why do them at all. In other words, let's be clear on the purpose before we jump into the activity.

WHY DO LLL ACTIVITIES?

The purpose is not the walk itself but rather what you see and hear on the walk and what you learn from your observations. Leaders should be encouraged to reflect on:

- What am I seeing here?
- What am I hearing (actively listening)?
- What have I learned from this experience?

> You are reflecting on what you have learned not only about a particular area or process but also about yourself.

You are reflecting on what you have learned not only about a particular area or process but also about yourself. Some useful questions to reflect on could be:

- Have I provided clarity on the business/team purpose?
- Have I encouraged and supported the ideal behaviours?
- Have I ensured that people are given systems and training that help them to do a great job and personally thrive?

A good Look, Listen and Learn activity should be used as an opportunity to receive feedback and understand what you personally need to change as a leader.

Before starting any LLL activity, always pause and ask: What is the purpose of this LLL activity? There are many reasons for doing an LLL. Here are just a few examples:

- to review improvement activity.

- to understand if people are being communicated with in an effective way.
- to understand if ideal behaviours are in place and being supported.
- to practice any of the hats: coach, teach, support, train, inspire, direct.
- to celebrate achievements and recognise great behaviours.

WHAT IS AN LLL ACTIVITY?

LLL activities are a learning process that leads to greater understanding. They are the foundation for further learning, development, and improvement, not only of the people we meet with but also of ourselves. They help distinguish between the process and the people.

However, they are not about checking up on people. To do them correctly, they require humility; for example, a leader checking whether people understand the company goals is actually about the leader checking the effectiveness of the deployment system, not the person they are talking to.

> LLLs provide the opportunity to learn firsthand what is really happening in the workplace.

When doing LLL, you are learning about the effectiveness of a particular system from the person who is a participant in it. It can often be a very humbling experience, as we will show in some of the case examples later in this chapter.

LLLs provide a way to help understand why the existing process may not be capable enough and help people understand that they are not to blame. It is about asking yourself the **5 Whys**, not the **5 Whos**.

LLLs provide the opportunity to learn firsthand what is really happening in the workplace. It is not about whether targets are being met but what support do people need to achieve those targets. You need to look at what is happening and listen to what people are saying both to you and to each other.

Ritsuo Shingo, who was President of the Shingo Institute, had a wonderful way to describe these activities: 'We should have big ears, big eyes and a little mouth'. If you are doing all the talking, then people stop thinking for themselves. As we will discuss later in this chapter, we cannot overestimate the power of listening.

Typical things we want to learn could include:

- Do people understand the business purpose and how they connect to it?
- Do people feel physically and psychologically safe?
- Do people feel they get the support they need to achieve their targets?
- Are people skilled in how to solve problems in a structured way that addresses the root cause?
- Are people living and breathing the organisation's ideal behaviours?
- Are our systems making it easy or harder to do the job in the right way?

All LLL activities should be followed by personal reflection time on what changes you might need to make personally to your ways of working, your leadership style, and your preconceptions.

One powerful activity is for leaders to review as a team what they have learned and what actions they need to take to improve themselves.

HOW?

When we talk to leaders about LLL activities, we often get a response along the lines of: 'I already do that—I visit the shop floor every day'. Whilst this is a good first step, it does not mean that there is an effective LLL process in place. Unfortunately, the activity can be driven by the wrong metric, such as a target of how many shop floor visits each leader must do but without any qualitative check on their effectiveness. In these scenarios, people are using a tool but risk undermining its effectiveness and credibility.

'What do I need to do to help people to do a great job and thrive in our organisation?'

How you do LLLs is critical to whether they are useful or not. You need to approach LLLs with the mindset that no one comes into work to deliberately do a bad job. Your role is to help employees to do a great job and you are undertaking LLLs to help understand what you need to do to support them. In effect, you are holding up a mirror to yourself and asking: 'What do I need to do to help people to do a great job and thrive in our organisation?'

LLL activities are an essential element to sustaining a culture of continuous improvement and, undertaken correctly, will support the personal development of leaders and colleagues across the organisation.

LLLs also provide lots of opportunities to practice recognition, kindness, listening, and coaching. These are three key activities that Warner, Greenlee and Butterworth (Why Care 2024) highlight as critical to supporting a positive workplace culture. A high-level summary of their findings is given below.

Recognition (Support Hat)

Many leaders struggle with recognition. A common attitude in many organisations can be summarized as 'Why do we need to recognise people for doing their job?' with the implication being that recognition is reserved for when people go above and beyond what is expected. Why not recognise that people are doing the right thing in the job we have asked them to do?

This is not about formal recognition programs linked to high value monetary reward; indeed, as highlighted by Marciano in his book *Why Carrots and Sticks Don't Work* (2010), these programs often drive the wrong behaviour.

Hines and Butterworth (*The Essence of Excellence* 2019) found that recognition was one of the key factors in high performing organisations. Recognition focused on ideal behaviours helps to embed those behaviours.

The value of Kindness (support hat)

The importance of kindness in the workplace is being increasingly understood. OC Tanner promotes '20 acts of random kindness', ranging from 'Give a shout-out to an employee during a meeting' to 'starting a kindness wall'. Several organisations have introduced 'kindness trees', where employees call out colleagues for recognition for acts of kindness. This in itself is seen as a further act of kindness.

Harvard Business Review (7 May 2021) published an article 'Don't underestimate the Power of kindness at work,' which highlights that:

A commitment to be kind can bring many important benefits. First, and perhaps most obviously, practicing kindness will be immensely helpful to our colleagues. Being recognised at work helps reduce employee burnout and absenteeism, and improves employee well-being, Gallup finds year after year in its surveys of U.S. workers.

> It is a critical enabler to build skills, reduce dependency, and thus free up leadership time from day to day activities.

Be a coach (coach hat)

We explored the coach hat in chapter 1 but expand on some key aspects here. Coaching develops other people so that they can think and act for themselves and realise their full potential. It is a critical enabler to build skills, reduce dependency, and thus free up leadership time from day to day activities.

Coaching is a conversation, or series of conversations, that one person has with another. A coaching conversation can last a few minutes or a couple of hours. A coaching conversation focuses on the other person, treating them as the expert. It consists of questions, listening and refection. You believe the person being coached can figure out what they need to do, and the conversation helps them to think and feel differently.

SKILLS OF A COACH

A coaching leader learns to adopt a less directive style when working with others and consciously asks open questions even when they think they know the answer. A coach will cultivate trust and safety and facilitate growth. There is a wide range of skills needed for effective coaching, but the two cornerstone coaching skills are active listening and asking questions.

A good coach will be very conscious of the pause, consider the person, consider the context approach we discussed in chapter 2.

Listening

Listening is vitally important in coaching conversations. Starr (2012) devotes a whole chapter in her book to listening but one of the key points she highlights is:

Listening is linked directly to our attention, and it starts with intending to listen, being focused and present, and concentrating. Really good listening means that we don't get distracted by our own thoughts and ideas; instead, we stay totally focused on the person, making them more important than ourselves (Starr 2012)

If you have any doubt about the power of listening, then pause and reflect on how you felt the last time you realised that someone was really listening to you.

Asking questions only works if we genuinely listen to the answers and respond to what we are hearing. A good question is simple, has a clear purpose and encourages learning and curiosity.

Some examples of good questions:

- Are there other approaches that you could use?
- What's on your mind?
- And what else?
- Why do you say that?
- What might the next step be?
- Why do you think that?
- What does good look like for you?

There are thousands of books and articles on how to coach and we can only give some essential pointers and tips for this critical skill in this book. Our key message is that all leaders need to develop this skill and continuously practice it to hone their skills. A few key tips are provided below:

Some key tips

- Summarise regularly—e.g. 'What you are saying is ...'
- The power of silence—don't jump in with another question whilst the coachee is still thinking about the last one.
- Active listening—look out for key words and phrases to hook into. Genuinely LISTEN.
- 80/20: the coachee should have most of the air time.
- Be present—show genuine interest. Don't try to multitask.
- Show respect.
- Don't chase a solution—focus on agreeing a next step.

If you want to continue to deepen your knowledge on coaching, then three books we highly recommend are:

- *Humble Inquiry* (2nd Edition) by Edgar and Peter Schein
- *The Coaching Habit* by Michael Bungar Stanier
- *Brilliant Coaching* by Julie Starr

Giving feedback during and after LLL events

An important aspect of the coach hat is giving feedback. This is a key skill to develop for every leader and it often poses some challenges caused primarily by two factors:

1. Ultimate carer (as discussed in Chapter 2) leadership tendencies, where we avoid giving feedback because we feel it could hurt the other person.
2. Low levels of psychological safety within a team.

Leaders with an ultimate carer leadership tendency will lead to avoid wearing the direct hat when needed. These leaders feel awkward about giving feedback because they are concerned about hurting the other person or worry about what the person receiving the feedback may do. This negative feeling about providing feedback leads them to refrain from giving feedback. This poses challenges to the success of LLL efforts within organisations, as the area visits by leadership can become more of a royal tour rather than a valuable learning experience for all parties involved.

Low levels of psychological safety also impact a leader's willingness to give feedback. Further, it affects the way people interpret the feedback. Providing feedback is seen as a career-limiting move in environments of low psychological safety. Being given feedback is seen as a threat or an attack, rather than being constructive and helpful.

Feedback is a two-way street: how we provide the feedback and how the other person takes feedback (see Figure 9.3 below).

FIGURE 9.3: Giving and receiving feedback.

Let's start with giving feedback in a coaching approach that provides the other person autonomy, allowing them to think and engage as in any good coaching conversation. We have created an acronym COACH to help remember and practice this approach:

C = Check in with the person by asking if you can chat. If they say no, ask when you can catch up with them.

O = Observation: Provide them specifics about what you observed – could be positive and/or negative. Be clear and concise and mention the potential impacts that could occur based on what you saw or heard.

A = Align with them, let them express their understanding of the situation and their thoughts, actively listen to their responses, and share your thoughts.

C = Choices: Ask them what choices or options they have to move forward and improve, based on the feedback.

H = How they will move on? what steps they will take to improve. Help them formulate actions they want to take.

COACH is a simple process for providing feedback. It is also influential in the coaching approach it takes, by engaging the other person in conversation through alignment, asking them what choices or options they have to move forward, and, finally, how they will move forward, the steps they will take by when, and what support they require.

Checking in and asking permission to have a conversation is a significant first step, as it shows respect for the other person and gives them autonomy. This calms emotions rather than just diving into some direct feedback, which can quickly shock and trigger a person's feelings.

Observation is all about being specific; don't be vague. What, when, who, and how—the more specific you can be with the observation feedback you provide, the more the other party will respect the information rather than dismiss it as purely an opinion.

The COACH feedback approach can be used for both positive and constructive feedback; it is not limited to a purely constructive situation. Again, being more specific with positive feedback makes it more meaningful and relevant.

CASE STUDY: YOU CAN'T FIX PROBLEMS FROM BEHIND YOUR DESK

(Support and Coach Hats)

I was facilitating an offsite workshop for a leadership team when a telephone call came from the site. The General Manager was in the workshop and asked if we could pause the session as they needed a quick discussion about the call. He shared the limited information he had received and got a barrage of questions and answers from across the room. There were lots of suggestions about how to fix the issue and who was to blame.

After several minutes, our author asked if it was okay to intervene. Smiling, the GM agreed. Our author pointed out that they were assuming they knew the answers while, in reality, they weren't certain about what had happened. We were only a five-minute drive away, so he asked if we could make this a LLL by doing activity and all go back to the site to where the issue had occurred to understand the facts.

We agreed the leaders would assume nothing, would ask some open questions, and listen carefully to the answers. The result was a revelation. They soon realised almost all their assumptions were incorrect and what had occurred was very different from what they thought. This understanding of the real issue enabled then to quickly agree on a plan to fix the issue, get immediate buy-in from all parties, and delegate the actions to the appropriate people.

It was a huge revelation for the team and far more insightful than any external training example he had planned to share. We went back to the training room and reflected on what we had learned—not about the problem but about the way the team typically addressed issues like this. They agreed that never again would they try and fix a problem from their office and adopted LLL as their standard approach.

CASE STUDY: LEARNING TO DO AN EFFECTIVE LLL ACTIVITY
(Support and Coach Hats)

A senior leader had been told they need to do two LLL activities a week. They were feeling some pressure because the target was not being met, so decided to venture out onto the shop floor and have a look around. They visited an area familiar to them and noticed that the team board had a lot of red ink. Many of the KPIs were below target and most of the projects behind plan.

TABLE 9.3: Look, Listen, Learn

First attempt	Consequences
The senior leader calls over the team leader and points at the board, angrily shouting about what a poor job the team leader is doing. He makes it clear that when he comes back next week he expects to see no red ink, with all targets being met and projects up to date. The whole exchange is entirely one way and takes no more than five minutes.	The team leader feels highly demotivated and passes this sentiment on to his team. He also is left with a poor opinion of the leader. The longer-term effect is that problems are now likely to be hidden, so the chances of fixing them are very low.

Second attempt	Consequences
Discussing this with one of the CI coaches and reflecting on what happened, the leader realises he could have handled it better. The next week he goes back to the same area. Little has changed and there is no visible improvement in any of the results on the board.	The team leader and team undertake some of the things they have been told to do but in a half-hearted, poorly executed way. The actions take no account of their knowledge of what's needed and, in many instances, do not address the team's real issues.

Second attempt	Consequences
He calls over to the team leader, who prepares himself for another telling off. But instead of shouting, the leader tells the team leader that he can see he needs some help and goes on the explain what the biggest problems are, what needs to be done by when, and exactly how to go about it before he visits again in a week's time.	The longer-term effect is that the team leader has been taught not to think for himself and, even if he does, he won't be allowed to implement his ideas. So why bother to suggest anything?
Again, the conversation is all one way, with no opportunity for the team leader to contribute and takes just over 10 minutes.	

Third attempt	Consequences
After another coaching session with one of the CI coaches, the senior leader is beginning to realise that he's still going about it the wrong way. He is not really looking and not listening, but he is learning a lot about himself.	The short-term result is that the team leader goes away all fired up, conveys this enthusiasm to the team and rapid progress is made.

Third attempt	Consequences
He approaches the team leader a week later and starts by asking how things are going and what the major two or three issues seem to be. The team leader responds by talking through three areas.	The longer-term result is that the team leader has been coached and will have a much better idea of what to do the next time a similar problem arises, and over time may also start to adopt a similar approach within his own team.
The senior leader takes one of these—the area that, due to his experience, he considers the most pressing—and asks what the team leader thinks might be done about it. The team leader responds with a few ideas. The senior leader selects the first one and asks how the team leader thinks it could be done.	The senior leader reflected on his learning and realised that although the third attempt took more time, the outcome was far better. He realised that if he didn't make the time to have good LLL conversations, he would never have time because he would be too busy firefighting the problems caused by his first two reactions.

Third attempt	Consequences
At the end of a 20-minute discussion, the team leader has a clear plan for his top two projects, what to do, and how to do it, which he has provided himself. The senior leader ends with a question about whether any more support is needed and agrees to check in again the next week.	

CASE STUDY: DEVELOPING LEADER STANDARD WORK BY INDRAJIT RAY AND PATRIZIA RANDO

(All 5 Hats)

How do leaders ensure that they consistently have time and energy to create the right environment? An environment where teams can support each other to do their best work and deliver their best outcomes? A major Australian Not-for-Profit organisation needed to create more clarity between fundraising programs to create a more connected portfolio. Many of the touchpoints and dependencies between teams were unclear, which caused gaps and overlaps, leading to inefficiency and rework.

The fundraising department needed a 'Chief of Staff' role to provide the overarching governance,

- to ensure better coordination between the teams,
- to bridge any siloed thinking,
- to be objective in the face of competing priorities,
- to drive a donor-led strategy.

The manager in the Supporter Engagement team was well positioned to step up into this role, but was too busy with the day-to-day activities, unplanned break-in work and consequent fire-fighting that existed in her team. There never seemed to be enough time to get everything done. She felt powerless to step away from supporting her team leader managing their team's operational work. The team leader was still growing in her role, and dependent on the manager for dealing with day-to-day problems and fixing front-line staff issues.

The manager had **taught** her team well, reinforcing training with Quick Reference Cards. She **supported** her team by helping them prioritise their work and meet their performance goals. But she was starting to recognise that she was operating at multiple levels of work. She was spending too much time on the team 'dance floor', trying to be across everything and fearful of letting go of the details. She was not spending enough time on her 'balcony', planning, inspiring and coaching. She needed the structure from Leader Standard Work (LSW) to diarise her 'sacred routines': her 1:1 coaching sessions, reminding the team of their purpose at huddles in front of the team's Visual Management Board, and actively listening to other stakeholders during cross-functional meetings (as part of an emerging Look, Listen, Learn practice).

She started to allocate deep focus time for planning and reflection. She delegated a lot more decision-making and operational detail to her team leader. She **inspired** her team leader to develop their own LSW, which internalised her own learning and held herself accountable to measure adherence to LSW. She **coached** her team leader to problem solve and **direct** front-line staff to refer to SOPs before asking questions and resolve supporter issues at source (where possible) rather than passing them on. She **supported** the team to take actions from team huddles and own them through to completion, whilst encouraging the team to give open and honest feedback.

With the additional capacity she created through LSW, the manager then became empowered to take on the additional responsibilities of a fundraising 'Chief of Staff'. She developed a 'firm but fair' persona, often able to role model ideal behaviours to other people-leaders, being data-led and decisive, whilst still being humble and respectful. Her changed mindset and leadership rhythm has enabled her to uplift her Look, Listen, Learn walk: to really understand the reality of how the fundraising teams were working and the active governance needed to uplift their ecosystem, to drive their strategic ambitions and hit their departmental goals. She did reflect however that the learning journey never stops; she continues to sharpen her LSW routines to ensure her best energy and focus gets the right things done, in the right way, for the best outcomes.

3 KEY TAKE AWAYS FROM THIS CHAPTER

1. Deliberately plan your time to focus on managing the culture you want.
2. LLL activities are a process of discovery—have an open mind and maintain curiosity throughout. It is never about validating preconceptions but about discovering what is going on.
3. Being a coaching leader is key to developing your people and freeing up your time.

ACTIVITY 9

Use the templates below to work out how much time you typically spend managing culture and set a goal to increase it. Using the PDCA example at the start of this chapter develop a plan to increase it.

TABLE 9.4: What can I stop doing?

Activities I can stop	Hours per week freed up

**TABLE 9.5: Time allocation plan to get to my goal
for time spent working on culture**

Activity	Hours per week

10

PURPOSE AND SYSTEMS DRIVE BEHAVIOUR

In chapter 9, we discussed the importance of dedicating considerable time to allocating time to manage the culture we want to see and the importance of using Look, Listen, Learn (LLL) activities to help us do this. In this chapter, we will explain how you can achieve your ideal culture by using key behavioural indicators (KBIs). These help us to ensure our systems are driving the behaviours we need.

When we think about our business systems (not our IT systems), we tend to think of continuous improvement as improving an individual system. However, while improving one system will have some localised benefit, it's likely to reduce the ability to achieve long-term sustainable results.

> # Leaders need to think about all the interconnecting systems of the organisation and work to improve them holistically.

One way to think about this is to use the analogy of the human body. Our bodies are an interconnected system with multiple dependencies. None of our organs are of any use, nor can they function, on their own. They are only of value as part of the overall system.

Leaders need to think about all the interconnecting systems of the organisation and work to improve them holistically to create high-performing sustainable results over time.

Let's take a look at this interconnectedness of systems in more detail. To uplift the performance of our continuous improvement system, we also need to think about the following systems (as examples and not limited to):

Reward and recognition system: To promote a high-performing culture of continuous improvement, you need to also have a strong reward and recognition system that will promote the ideal behaviours you need across the enterprise that will drive that improvement. Failure to recognise or reward those who are continually looking to improve their daily work will not get you the long-term results you require.

Strategy and behaviour deployment system: Your continuous improvement system must be intrinsically linked to the strategy of the organisation so that the teams are working on the right activities that will impact the overall business goals. It should also consider the ideal behaviours needed to achieve the strategic goals so that you can manage

KBIs not just KPIs. Improving the continuous improvement system of an enterprise with a different viewpoint or strategy will eventually fail.

Leader standard work system: Building or making changes to an improvement system also needs to have an interconnected strong leader standard work system. Leaders need to apply a standard to how they use their coach, support, and teach hats in a consistent manner, in conjunction with the reward and recognition system, so that the teams receive the development and recognition they deserve to drive the improvement outcomes.

People system: To have an effective and efficient improvement system, you need people working within the system to have the capabilities to be able to perform. They need to have a strong onboarding, training, and development system in place so that leaders can again use their teach and coach hats to ensure that they continue to learn and grow each day.

Change and communications system: Even a good continuous improvement system will eventually fall flat without an effective change and communications system (we spoke speak about this system in chapter 7). Essentially, you need to be able to create a strong change and communications system to enable your frontline teams to absorb the sheer volume of change that they encounter in today's world of VUCA. Any improvements you make to any of your systems need to be communicated succinctly so that your frontline teams can understand what is required of them.

Health and safety system (HSE): The health and safety of your people (including psychological safety) is your number one priority as a leader, so making any improvements to your systems requires you to ensure that

As you can see, a change to one system can necessitate improvements to other systems to create sustainable results.

you haven't inadvertently negatively impacted any HSE controls. Change that impacts your people's health and safety needs to be communicated effectively using your change and communications system.

As you can see, a change to one system can necessitate improvements to other systems to create the sustainable results needed to drive the business vision or purpose. To do this, you need to apply a rigorous Plan, Do, Check, Act (PDCA) cycle to all your system changes (see Figure 10.1 below).

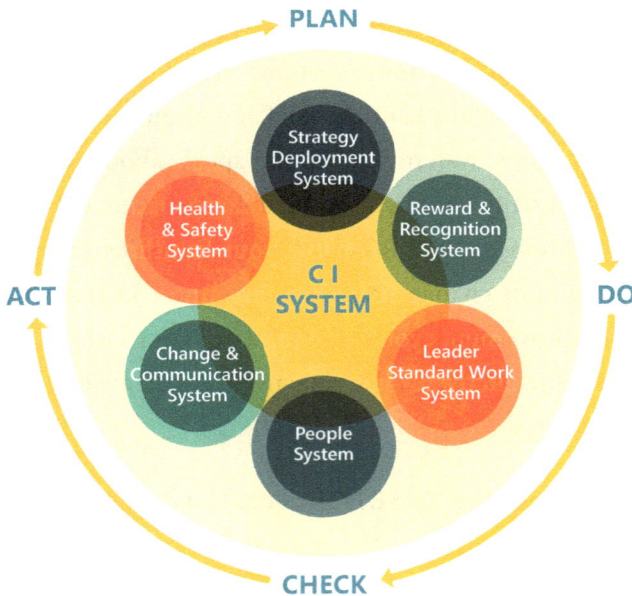

FIGURE 10.1: Interdependent systems example.

All of our systems drive behaviour. We need to proactively manage these systems to ensure they drive the behaviours that demonstrate our desired culture. This is not a one-off exercise. It takes time and constant attention.

Managing culture is like cultivating a beautiful garden. We can spend enormous time and effort getting everything to look just as we desire but

> All of our systems drive behaviour.

without constant care and attention it quickly goes to ruin. Weeds grow, things go out of shape and, within weeks, something that took years to establish and flourish is unrecognisable.

We find it useful to think of ourselves as gardeners constantly nurturing the culture every day so that it can strengthen and flourish. LLL activities are key to doing this but are not enough on their own.

IDEAL RESULTS REQUIRE IDEAL BEHAVIOURS

Let's be honest, you don't spend a lot of time managing culture just because it's a nice thing to do. True, it creates a much more enjoyable place to work and it's very rewarding to see the passion and commitment created across the organisation as a result of this focus. However, this can only continue to thrive if we are delivering the results that the organisation needs to be successful.

The Shingo Institute teaches that ideal results require ideal behaviours but what does this mean? An ideal result is something that's sustainable and delivers value to our customers, the organisation, and our people. Ideal behaviours are actions that support the delivery of ideal results.

An ideal result is something that's sustainable and delivers value to our customers, the organisation, and our people.

Sure, we can get good results in the short term with poor behaviours, but this is not sustainable. There are always negative consequences of this, even if they are not immediately obvious in the short term. Some common examples we see are people slashing maintenance or people development budgets to increase short-term profits, which often results in increased machine breakdowns, low morale, and high staff turnover.

SYSTEMS AND PURPOSE DRIVE BEHAVIOUR

Another key insight from the Shingo Institute is that systems and purpose drive behaviour. By *system*, we do not mean the IT systems, but rather the core operating systems of the organisation. These typically include the strategy deployment system; the continuous improvement system; the recruitment, learning, and development system; and the operations system. IT systems are often the automation of these core systems.

What many leaders miss is that an organisation's systems drive behaviour and often not the behaviour you wanted or expected (see Figure 10.2 below).

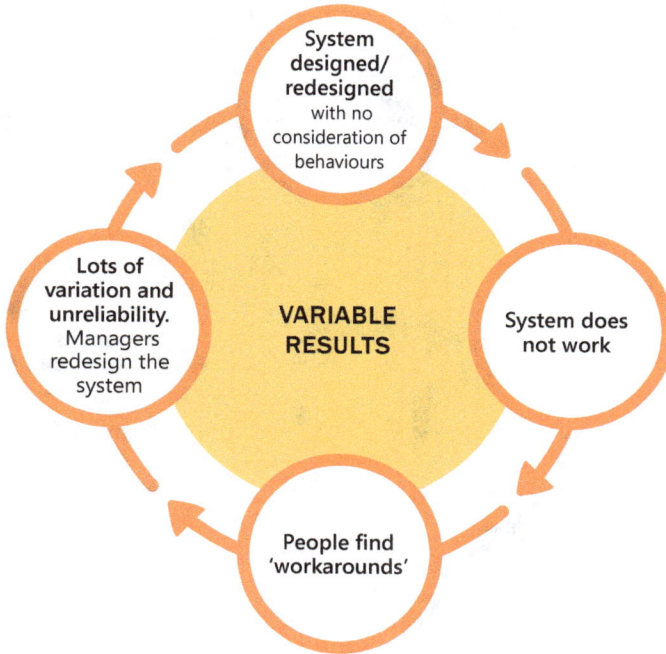

FIGURE 10.2: Systems drive behaviour. (Adapted from *Why Bother?* **Butterworth, et al, 2022)**

This is often not the result of deliberate design. In most cases, it happens because we have not really considered the behaviours, we need before designing the system. Just by pausing and asking a few questions and applying a PDCA cycle (See Figure 10.3) we will get a very different system. These questions are:

1. What is our purpose for this system?
2. What behaviours do we need to deliver this purpose?
3. How could we measure these behaviours (KBIs)?

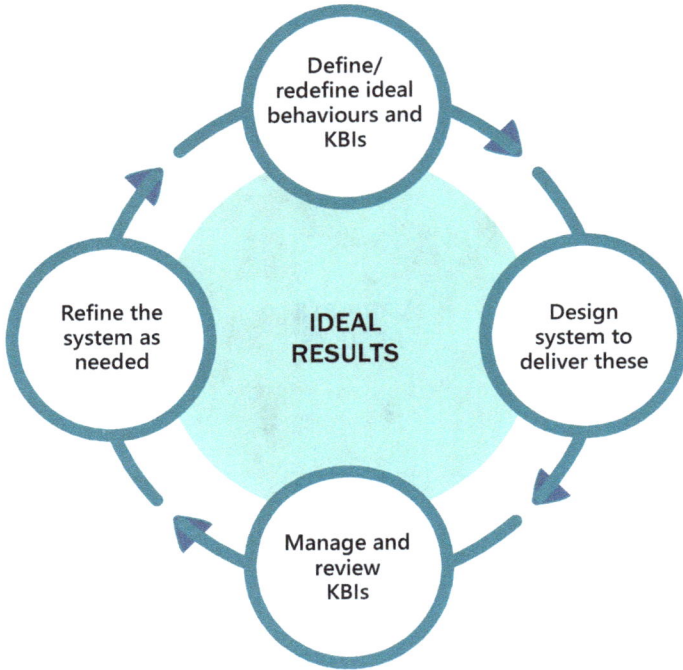

FIGURE 10.3: Designing systems with clarity on purpose and behaviours. (Adapted from *Why Bother?* Butterworth, et al, 2022)

Unfortunately, we rarely get the chance to design a system from scratch and even when we do, we need a way to check whether it's driving the behaviours we need. This is where KBIs come in.

KEY BEHAVIOURAL INDICATORS

We tend to put a lot of leadership effort into reviewing and managing KPIs. The problem with this is that they only tell us what has already happened, and we then have to work out how to fix something that's already gone off track. Leading an organisation in this way is like trying to drive a car only looking through the rear-view mirror.

To get ideal results, we need ideal behaviours. To measure the ideal behaviours we need KBI's. KPIs tell us what has already happened but KBIs tell us what is likely to happen if we don't take action. They are a very effective form of lead indicator (see Figure 10.4 below)

FIGURE 10.4: KPIs look backwards. KBIs look ahead.

KBIs tell us if we have the ideal behaviours in place that will deliver ideal results (see Figure 10.5 below).

FIGURE 10.5: KBIs tell us if we have the ideal behaviours in place that will deliver ideal results. (Adapted from *Why Bother?* **Butterworth, et al, 2022**)

KBIs are measuring whether the behaviours we want are in place. However, from a leadership perspective, the important thing about KBIs is that they are indicators of a potential issue with one or more of our systems. In other words, KBIs are not just a measure of behaviours; they are really measuring the effectiveness of the system and should support the PDCA cycle of improving the system.

HOW TO USE KBIs

KBIs can be used in many ways at all levels across an organisation. You probably have some already in place (such as employee engagement survey results) but might not class them as KBIs. Specifically identifying KBI's as separate to KPI's is a very useful distinction to make. It means you can then review how much time you are spending looking backward reviewing KPIs compared to how much time you are spending looking forward reviewing KBIs.

> Don't start with asking, 'What should our KBIs be?'

Don't start with asking, 'What should our KBIs be?' Instead, agree on the purpose you are trying to achieve. This could be a specific outcome you need from a system, a short-term goal, a long-term cultural shift, or a specific behaviour or new habit you want to embed.

Once you have this clear, you can define one or more key behaviours that are required to achieve this. Now, you ask yourself, 'What could the KBI(s) be to measure that behaviour?'

Examples of how to use KBIs

- The leadership team (or any team in the organisation) agrees on the behaviours they want to see at their meetings. Agenda time is allocated at the end of each meeting to review, 'How did we perform against our behaviours, with good and/or not so good examples?'

  The team then decides to rate the meeting in relation to the agreed behaviours. Green (good), amber (could be better), or red (we forgot all about them). This is noted either on the minutes or team visual board, with a couple of agreed actions that are reviewed at the start of the next meeting.

  It will seem a little clunky at first, but it will quickly become a new habit that will help embed new behaviours. Just talking about the behaviours helps bring them to life and deepen understanding.

- Create a high-level 'systems map' for each of your key systems and decide which KBIs need to be measured to ensure the system is driving the right behaviours needed to achieve the KPIs.

- KBIs are very powerful if reviewed and managed on a team's visual board. Some organisations have matured to the level where the KBIs are the main thing the team discusses because they know that if the KBIs are achieved then the results will be on target.

Examples of specific KBIs

- A hospital wanted to reduce infection rates. For years they reported the number of infections and it stayed higher than desired. They determined that one of the biggest drivers of reducing infections was people properly and frequently washing their hands. So they introduced a KBI on frequency of hand washing which was measured with a simple electronic (app) confirmation system. Once this was up and running, infection rates started to reduce significantly.

- One manufacturer was consistently achieving 96% *on time in full* delivery but could not achieve the 99% target. They undertook LLL activities across the site and learned that although *on time in full* was on every team's visual board and reviewed at every huddle, few people outside of the logistics department felt they could do anything to influence it. They set up a work group to investigate and arranged for teams to measure the one thing they could do that impacted *on time in full*. All the team in production shifted the measure to ensuring adherence to the daily schedule they had been given. This drove ownership and connection to something people could influence themselves and led to a change in attitude and behaviour. With a few months, *on time in full* was at 99% and often 100%.

- One team at a financial services organisation wanted to ensure they were providing a good service to their internal customers. They had this as a KBI on their visual board and decided to invite a customer representative to their huddle meeting twice a month. At the end of the meeting, the customer was asked: 'Did we discuss the things that are important to you?' If a clear 'yes', then the KBI was coded green; if 'yes, but', then orange; if 'no', then red. In all three cases, the supplementary question was, 'What do we need to improve?'

- Several organisations have found it useful to implement a simple KBI to drive a habit of improvement. At the basic level, this could be number of continuous improvement ideas per team per week.

- As we discussed in chapter 9, shifting leaders' time allocation to focus on culture is critical. A simple KBI would measure what percentage of their week leaders allocate to managing culture.
- Several organisations measure the number of recognitions for behaviour given by the leadership team each week. This is a powerful KBI as it not only encourages leaders to do more recognition, which is highly motivating for people, but also reinforces the desired behaviours across the organisation.

MATURING KBIS

One important thing to consider about KBIs is that we need to mature them over time. Generally, they will go through three stages. This concept was put forward by Peter Hines in the book Why Bother (Butterworth et al 2021).

Stage 1: Are we doing it? Getting the behaviour established.

Stage 2: How often are we doing it? Number of/frequency to ensure it's an embedded habit.

Stage 3: What's the quality/effectiveness? To ensure it's really adding value not just ticking a box.

Here are some specific examples to illustrate this.

Example of increasing the application of the coach hat

A large financial services team wanted to expand on the use of the coach hat by leaders and decided one of the activities to focus on was one-on-one discussions. The expectation was set that every leader should do one-on-one discussions with each of their direct reports. The Stage 1 KBI was simply, have you done a one-on-one meeting with each of your direct reports? Yes or No. This started changing behaviours but had mixed results, as some leaders did them weekly, others monthly and, in some cases, quarterly.

So, the Stage 2 KBI was that every leader had to do a 30-minute one-on-one review with each of their direct reports twice a month. This created a clear standard for the expected behaviour and was easily tracked, as people completed a simple tracker confirming if they had received their one-on-one. The habit was soon established and after three months most people were having one-on-one conversations twice a month. However, it became apparent that while some people found them useful, others seemed to think they were a waste of time.

The Stage 3 KBI was a radical step forward. The organisation regularly used the nett promotor score system with external customers and decided to apply it to the internal one-on-one discussions. They changed the question on the one line tracker to, 'How valuable did you find your one-on-one meeting?' on a scale of 1 to 5. Analysis of the results provided insights for further improvements to the one-on-one system. For example, it highlighted which leaders needed coaching support on how to do more effective one-on-ones, as well as the need for clear standards around the structure of the meetings. It was communicated to everyone and constantly reinforced that the purpose of the KBI was not to check up on people but to understand how to continuously improve the effectiveness of the system.

Example of increasing the application of the inspire hat

Stage 1: Number of CI ideas.

Stage 2: Percentage of CI ideas implemented.

Stage 3: Percentage of CI ideas implemented aligned to company goals.

Example of increasing the application of the support hat

Stage 1: Number of 5 Whys problem-solving activities completed

Stage 2: Number of 5 Whys problem-solving activities completed per team reviewed by the manager with the team.

Stage 3: Number of problems that have reoccurred after the 5 Whys exercise has been completed and countermeasures implemented (ideally zero).

Example of increasing the application of the coaching, inspire, and support hats

Stage 1: Number of LLL activities per leader

Stage 2: Percentage of achievement of the target number of LLL activities per leader per week.

Stage 3: Number of peer reviews undertaken by leaders on lessons learned about how to do better LLL activities.

FREEDOM WITHIN A FRAMEWORK

It's easy to fall into the trap of trying to manage everything and make every decision. This often stems from a desire to make sure everything is done just how we would do it in an attempt to ensure quality. Unfortunately, by doing this we constrain our people and overburden ourselves.

A better alternative is to use the leadership hats to help us to build our people's capabilities so that we can delegate decision making and improvement. We cannot have anarchy, but we need a level of controlled freedom. We need to ensure that our people are not constrained or even just compliant but that they are committed.

> It's easy to fall into the trap of trying to manage everything and make every decision.

This is where the concept of freedom within a framework comes into play. One way to think about our systems is that they provide the framework for our people to work within. If the framework is too controlling and requires everything to be approved by senior leaders, then it constrains our people. They are forced to comply (even when they know a better way) and will generally be disengaged as a result (see Figure 10.6 below).

FREEDOM WITHIN A FRAMEWORK

Constrained • • • • • • • • • • • Committed

FIGURE 10.6: Freedom within a framework—unleash people potential.

We need to think of our systems as providing a framework that can give people the freedom to act on their own initiative but still provide clear boundaries about what is acceptable and what is not. We want our systems to unleash the full potential of all our people. For example, the widest level of freedom might be don't do anything that's unsafe or illegal or that will have a negative impact on the customer.

In this environment, our systems and procedures represent the current best known way to undertake a particular task. If people can think of a better way,

> Think of our systems as providing a framework that can give people the freedom to act on their own initiative.

If we make the improvement system too hard, then ideas will wither and die and people will remain constrained.

then they can follow a simple (but still controlled) improvement process.

If we make the improvement system too hard, then ideas will wither and die and people will remain constrained.

A quotation from Richard Sheridan (Sheridan 2015), CEO and chief storyteller of Menlo Innovations, provides a good high-level description of what we can expect to see in organisations that have built a culture of continuous improvement:

Our team members working together with a spirit that is lifted, with a resolve that is focused on solving problems at work, with a heart that says, 'I am going to collaborate with the people around me.'

CASE STUDY: FREEDOM WITHIN A FRAMEWORK

(The Inspire and Support Hats)

One supermarket chain with over 150 stores nationally, had spent several years shifting the culture from one of command and control to one of creating freedom for employees to make improvements. As the culture improved and the trust between leaders and employees grew, the boundaries of freedom incrementally increased. This did not everywhere at once, but as a store reached a certain level of cultural maturity the boundaries became as simple as 'do what you think is right for the customer but don't do anything illegal or unsafe'.

I was undertaking a cultural maturity assessment at one of the flagship stores. This consisted of observing many team discussions and problem-solving sessions and interviewing a wide range of people across all roles. The company's purpose was *to make our lives and customers' lives better every day*. This was prominently displayed on all visual management boards and discussed at every team meeting, with people sharing any action they had done in the last few days to help deliver purpose. It was a fantastic way to bring the purpose to life and help people connect to it personally.

One of the team members being interviewed was a young check-out operator who was in her first job since leaving school. When our author asked if she had any recent examples of how she had contributed to delivering the purpose, she told a remarkable story.

'Well last week one of our regular customers was trying to pay for her shopping. She has three young children and it's always a bit stressful for her to keep them under control at the checkout. When she counted out her cash to pay for the shopping she was $1.20 short. She looked like she was going to burst into tears and asked me to take something back so she had enough money. It was only $1.20 so I gave it to her. She was so grateful; it made me feel good.'

The thing was, she hadn't taken the money out of the register but used her own. Also, she had not shared the story publicly as she didn't think it was worth mentioning. When I shared her story (with her permission) with the senior leadership, they were bowled over. There was a lot of reflection and discussion, with most people celebrating that this had happened but with a few others wary of the wider implications. 'We can't let this become the norm or everyone will expect us to do it' was one minority view.

Eventually, they agreed that where the culture and trust were at the right levels, this was exactly how they wanted their people to behave. But with one significant difference: they didn't want staff to use their own money. So, the freedom framework was made even wider for those stores at the highest level of cultural maturity and each check-out operator had a discretionary allowance if they felt it was needed. It is rarely used but the fact that they are trusted in this way further boosts engagement and commitment. People are inspired and supported to think for themselves.

KEY TAKE AWAYS

1. Define the behaviours you want to see to deliver your goals.
2. Design systems that enable these behaviours.
3. Manage behaviours with KBIs and apply the PDCA cycle to continuously improve the processes and behaviours.

ACTIVITY 10

In chapter 4 we asked you to think about some ideal behaviours and which hats to wear to support them. For this exercise, please review those behaviours you identified for leaders, list them in the table below and then have a go at some potential KBIs to measure the behaviour you want to see.

TABLE 10.1: Activity 10 . Define Ideal behaviour and potential KBI's.

Ideal Behaviour	KBI's

11

SUMMARY AND SELF-ASSESSMENT EXERCISES

Our intention with this book has been to share our experiences of the key skills demonstrated by leaders who have embedded cultures of excellence into their organisations. We have explored the importance of understanding your core belief system and why it's important to pause and reflect before we respond. Context is critical but we will be more effective if we ensure that humility, trust, and respect underpin all our daily activities as leaders.

There is no substitute for learning by doing.

We've discussed the importance of purpose from a personal and organisational perspective and how critical it is to connect these. We've also explained why it's critical to focus on the individuals in your team and provided an easy-to-use formula to help with this.

While we have focused on the importance of behaviours, we have also shared our experience that these need to be intentionally supported by the systems in your organisation. You need to continuously improve these systems to ensure they are driving the ideal behaviours you need to create thriving individuals and a thriving organisation.

While we hope that all these examples provide a wealth of shared experiences that can be adapted and applied within your own organisation, there is no substitute for learning by doing.

> Remember to celebrate your progress and congratulate yourself on your achievements.

This is why we have provided the 5 Hats as a simple way to think about how to apply and practice these essential skills. The *Look, Listen and Learn* approach is one of the best ways to apply the skills and practice the application of the different hats.

In the tables below, you will find two self-assessments. The first one summarises the essential skills needed by the adaptive leader. The second one provides a self-assessment on the application of the 5 Hats of the adaptive leader.

These are not pass or fail assessments—there are no wrong answers. The intention is to help you understand where you are today and to come up with a simple plan to help you to progress in the areas you consider most important. We hope they provide a framework that you can come back to and review on a regular basis.

Remember to celebrate your progress and congratulate yourself on your achievements.

ACTIVITY 11.1

Place a tick in the box that most closely matches your view of yourself. If you feel comfortable doing so, it's always a good idea to sense check your self-assessment with a trusted colleague.

LEADING EXCELLENCE

Leader Self Assessment

	1	2	3	4	5
I have a good understanding of my Core Belief System	○	○	○	○	○
I am skilled at pausing before I react, considering the person and context surrounding them before I act	○	○	○	○	○
I demonstrate Humility, Trust and Respect in all my interactions	○	○	○	○	○
I have a deep understanding of my personal purpose and how this connects to the organisation purpose	○	○	○	○	○
I can clearly articulate my organisations purpose and help other people to connect to this	○	○	○	○	○
I am skilled at truly understanding every individual in my team and their intrinsic and extrinsic interference	○	○	○	○	○
I focus the majority of my time on proactively managing culture	○	○	○	○	○
I have a rigorous internal and external networking system in place	○	○	○	○	○
I frequently undertake Look, Listen and Learn activities to nurture our culture	○	○	○	○	○
I have a deep understanding of how systems drive behaviour and how to use KBIs	○	○	○	○	○

Leading Excellence Key Skills

1. Early days
2. Have a good level of awareness and am willing to have a go
3. Feel confident about this and I am practising
4. I am recognised as doing this really well
5. I lead by example and coach others in this

FIGURE 11.1: Adaptive leader skills—Leader self-assessment.

ACTIVITY 11.2

Now pick a maximum of three areas where you would like to improve and commit to one thing you will do to move towards the next level.

TABLE 11.1: Adaptive leader skills—Personal action plan.

Key skill	Action	Target completion date	What help do I need?

ACTIVITY 11.3

Place a tick in the box that most closely matches your view of yourself. If you feel comfortable doing so, it's always a good idea to sense check your self-assessment with a trusted colleague.

We asked you to do a self-assessment at the end of chapter 2 and have repeated here so that you can review your progress and create an action plan for further self-development.

Table 11.2: The 5 Hats of the adaptive leader self-assessment.

ADAPTIVE LEADER HAT	MATURITY				
	1	2	3	4	5
Direct					
Support					
Teach					
Inspire					
Coach					

1. Need to get this hat
2. Started to practice
3. Use regularly
4. Recognised as proficient
5. Lead by example and coach others

ACTIVITY 11.4

Now pick a maximum of two hats you would like to improve and commit to some action you will do to move towards the next level.

TABLE 11.3: Identify the hats you want to develop and key actions you are going to take.

Hat	Action	Target completion date	What help do I need?

Remember, these are not a one-off exercise, and we recommend you regularly review your progress using the PDCA cycle.

REFERENCES

Chapter 1

Gallup Employee Engagement 2023. https://www.gallup.com/394373/indicator-employee-engagement.aspx

Sutherland et al 2020 2020-Scrum-Guide-US. https://scrumguides.org/

Sutherland 2019. *The Art of Doing Twice the Work and Half the Time*. Random House Business London.

Blanchard 1982 *The One Minute Manager*. William Morrow & Co New York.

Duhigg 2014 *The Power of Habit*. Random House USA Inc New York.

Heifetz et al 2019 The Practice of Adaptive Leadership. Harvard Business Review Press Massachusetts

Chapter 2

Collison 2017 Your Learner Talent: A Journey From Ignorance to Competence. Gallup https://www.gallup.com/cliftonstrengths/en/250001/learner-talent-journey-ignorance-competence.aspx

Bono 1985 *Six Thinking Hats: An Essential Approach to Business Management*. Little, Brown, & Company New York.

Banoub 2022 The 7 hats of great leadership. LinkedIn. https://www.linkedin.com/pulse/7-hats-great-leadership-paul-banoub/

Taylor 2019 the Four Hats of Leadership. New Insights Press

Young 2023 A Leaders Hats; The Five Main Hats Leaders must wear.....
and wear well. LinkedIn https://www.linkedin.com/pulse/
leaders-hats-5-main-all-must-wear-well-andre-young/

Duhigg 2014 *The Power of Habit*. Random House USA Inc New York.

Collins 2001 *Good to Great* Random House London.

Ebbinghaus 1913 *Memory: A Contribution to Experimental Psychology*.
Teachers College Columbia University New York.

Sutherland 2019. *The Art of Doing Twice the Work and Half the Time*.
Random House Business London.

Warner, Greenlee, Butterworth *Why Care? How Thriving Individuals
Create Thriving Cultures of Continuous Improvement Within
Organisations*. 2024 Routledge NY

Frey et al 2013 Keys to Literacy International Reading Association.
https://keystoliteracy.com/wp-content/uploads/2017/08/
frey_douglas_and_nancy_frey-_gradual_release_of_responsibility_
intructional_framework.pdf

Gallagher 1983 The Instruction of Reading Comprehension.
Contemporary Educational Psychology

Hehir 2020 The Last Dance. ESPN FILMS and NETFLIX

Whitmore 1992 Coaching for Performance. Nicholas Brealey
Publishing London

Chapter 3

Shingo Institute Three insights of Enterprise Excellence. https://
shingo.org/shingo-model/ John Huntsman School of Business

Oxford University Press 2024 Organisational Culture Definition.
https://www.oxfordreference.com/display/10.1093/
acref/9780199234899.001.0001/acref-9780199234899-e-
4582#:~:text=organizational%20culture%20(corporate%20
culture)&text=The%20values%2C%20customs%2C%20
rituals%2C,new%20members%20of%20the%20organization.

Gallup Employee Engagement 2023. https://www.gallup.com/394373/indicator-employee-engagement.aspx

Williams 2023 *The Connected Species. How the evolution of the human brain can save the world* Rowman & Littlefield London.

Scandar 2024 Core Belief System Development Contribution.

Andrews 2023 *The Wolf you Feed*. Macmillan Australia Sydney.

Chapter 4

Warner, Greenlee, Butterworth *Why Care? How Thriving Individuals Create Thriving Cultures of Continuous Improvement Within Organisations*. 2024 Routledge NY

Shingo Model Handbook. Available as a free download from www.Shingo.org

Chapter 5

John Seddon *I want you to cheat* 1992 Vangaurd Publishing Ltd

Chapter 6

James Kerr Legacy August 2015: *What the All Blacks Can Teach Us about the Business of Life*. Constable, London

Chapter 7

Value Driver Tree (VDT). First used by DuPont in the 1920's

Hines et al 1998. Value Stream Management. The International Journal of Logistics Management Vol. 9 Iss1 pp25-42

Chapter 8

W.Edwards Deming. The Deming Institute .www.deming.org. Source: quotes.deming.org/10091

Chapter 9

Peter Hines and Chris Butterworth, *The Essence of Excellence* 2019 S A Partners, Caerphilly

Chris Butterworth et al 2021 *Why Bother? How and Why to Access your Continuous Improvement Culture*. Routledge, New York

Warner, Greenlee, Butterworth *Why Care? How Thriving Individuals Create Thriving Cultures of Continuous Improvement Within Organisations*. 2024 Routledge NY

Paul L. Marciano *Why Carrots and Sticks Don't Work* 2010, McGraw Hill

Humble Inquiry (2nd Edition) by Edgar and Peter Schein Berrett-Koehler Publishers, Oakland

Brilliant Coaching by Julie Starr

O.C Tanner Vale of Kindness . www.octanner.com

Harvard Business Review (7 May 2021) published an article 'Don't underestimate the Power of kindness at work,'

The Coaching Habit by Michael Bungar Stanier Box of Crayons Press, Toronto

Chapter 10

Richard Sheridan, 2015 Joy Inc. Menlo Innovations, Ann Arbo, MI

You can find additional resources on www.leadingexcellencebook.com, including a free download of a *Leading Excellence* Maturity Assessment.

www.ingramcontent.com/pod-product-compliance
Lightning Source LLC
Chambersburg PA
CBHW061238220326
41599CB00028B/5468